Ghulam Murshid
48 Dovedale Avenue,
Ilford, Essex IG5 0QF UK

Family History

Family History

Janaki Agnes Penelope Majumdar
(née Bonnerjee)

Edited and with an Introduction by
Antoinette Burton

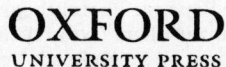

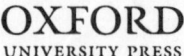
OXFORD
UNIVERSITY PRESS

YMCA Library Building, Jai Singh Road, New Delhi 110 001

Oxford University Press is a department of the University of Oxford. It furthers the
University's objective of excellence in research, scholarship, and education
by publishing worldwide in

Oxford   New York

Auckland   Bangkok   Buenos Aires   Cape Town   Chennai
Dar es Salaam   Delhi   Hong Kong   Istanbul   Karachi   Kolkata
Kuala Lumpur   Madrid   Melbourne   Mexico City   Mumbai   Nairobi
São Paulo   Shanghai Taipei   Tokyo   Toronto

Oxford is a registered trade mark of Oxford University Press
in the UK and in certain other countries

Published in India
By Oxford University Press, New Delhi

© Oxford University Press 2003

The moral rights of the author have been asserted
Database right Oxford University Press (maker)

First Published 2003

All rights reserved. No part of this publication may be reproduced,
or transmitted in any form or by any means, electronic or mechanical,
including photocopying, recording or by any information storage and
retrieval system, without permission in writing from Oxford University Press.
Enquiries concerning reproduction outside the scope of the above should be
sent to the Rights Department, Oxford University Press, at the address above

You must not circulate this book in any other binding or cover
and you must impose this same condition on any acquirer

ISBN   019 566360 8

Typeset by Le Studio Graphique, Delhi 110 017
in AGaramond 11/13
Printed by Rajshree Photolithographers
Published by Manzar Khan, Oxford University Press
YMCA Library Building, Jai Singh Road, New Delhi 110 001

*In memoy of Amar Singh
and his beloved 'Granny'*

Acknowledgements

Without the generosity and graciousness of the late Amar Singh and his wife Sally, Janaki Majumdar's *Family History* might have remained unavailable to a more general public. I am deeply appreciative of their support, especially during difficult times. I hope that the extended Bonnerjee-Majumdar clan will find 'Granny' here in ways they recognize from family lore or remember from personal experience.

Barbara Ramusack and George Robb read the introduction and offered valuable feedback. I am also profoundly indebted to Geraldine Forbes, who also read the introduction, guided me on the translation of many Bengali words, expressions and idioms, and—as is typical—was tireless in her support of this project.

Thanks, too, to Paul and Nicholas, who help me every day to appreciate the power of family histories.

Editor's Note

In contrast with what Muchu Chaudhuri wrote about his great-aunt's other writing (*see* Introduction), *Family History* needed very little editing. The chapter headings and Parts are as they were. I have occasionally made minor changes in the punctuation and syntax, and cut out some very short sections (mainly to effect smooth transitions where pages were missing, and then only rarely). I have also added explanatory notes to those that Janaki herself had entered. There is evidence in the original manuscript that there was a second pen at work making very small corrections over the main text (though there are no more than 5–7 instances of this in the whole manuscript). More frequently, it is clear that Janaki went over the manuscript herself after it was complete (or after writing certain sections) and scribbled notes about what to add, etc., including the incomplete sections at the very end of *Family History*.

Contents

Introduction by Antoinette Burton   *xiii*

Janaki Majumdar's *Family History*

Part 1
The Majumdar Family

1.1 P.M.'s Ancestry 5
1.2 Early Days 7
1.3 Religious Influences 10
1.4 College Days: Calcutta and Creek Row 12
1.5 First Marriage to Wife's Death (1894–9) 14
1.6 Work at Gidhaur (1900–4) 15
1.7 Student Days in England (1904–7) 17
1.8 Friends and Acquaintances 19
1.9 Experiences in South Africa 21
1.10 Return to India (1908) 23
1.11 Work in Calcutta 26
1.12 Sisters and Relatives 28

Part 2

The Bonnerjee Family

2.1 Ancestry of Womesh Chunder Bonnerjee: His Parents and Early Life (1844–64) *35*

2.2 Hemangini Bonnerjee: Her Parents, Early Life and Marriage (1849–59) *38*

2.3 W.C. Bonnerjee in England (1864–8) *42*

2.4 Return to Calcutta *46*

2.5 Beginnings of a Life in English Style (1868–74) *48*

2.6 Hemangini's First Visit to England (1874–5) *51*

2.7 Kidderpore House, Calcutta (1876–84) *55*

2.8 6 Park Street, Calcutta (1885) *59*

2.9 The Founding of the Congress (1885) *61*

2.10 Family Life at 6 Park Street *65*

2.11 Settling in England (1888) *68*

2.12 Kidderpore, Croydon *71*

2.13 Notes by Mrs Arthur Alexander: The Bonnerjee Family *75*

2.14 Life in Croydon: The Final Sorrow (1890) *80*

2.15 College Friends: Nellie's and Shelley's Engagements (1892) *84*

2.16 Shelley's Wedding (11-10-1893) *87*

2.17 Visit to India (1893–5) *89*

2.18 Life in Calcutta *91*

2.19 Birth of Kew (1894), Return to England (1895) *94*

2.20 Miss Neligan *97*

2.21 School Days (1895–9) *101*

2.22 My Father's Retirement and Work at the Privy Council (1902–5) *104*

2.23 College Days (1904–7) *108*

2.24 Death of W.C. Bonnerjee (21-7-06) *110*

2.25 Remaining Years of Hemangini Bonnerjee's Life (1906–10) *113*

Part 3
Early Married Life

3.1   6 Park Street Again (1908) *121*
3.2   Early Married Life (1909–10) *123*
3.3   Life at Elysium Row *126*
3.4   Visits of Nellie and Susie to India *129*
3.5   Early School Days: P.M.'s Activities *133*
3.6   Goodbye to Calcutta (1919–20) *136*

Notes 139

Select Bibliography 145

Introduction

Janaki Agnes Penelope Majumdar (1886–1963) was the daughter of one of India's most famous nationalist fathers—W.C. Bonnerjee (1844–1906), the first president of the Indian National Congress and one of the founders of modern Indian nationalism. Her *Family History* is an eloquent testimonial to the opportunities and challenges which that privileged position offered her as she grew up in two fin-de-siècle worlds, India and Britain. It is also a rare and remarkable evidence of the effects that Indian nationalist ideologies could have on the intricacies of middle-class family life in the late Victorian era, when talk of companionate marriage, the education of girls, and the benefits of 'modern' household practices were central to the articulation of what historian Mrinalini Sinha has called the emergent 'Indian modern'.[1] Written in 1935, during commemorations of the 50th anniversary of the founding of the INC, Majumdar's *Family History* tells the story of how her mother Hemangini (1849–1910) worked to create and maintain family households in both London and Calcutta which could serve as models of domestic reform for the *bhadralok* community at large. This transnational existence, and the sorrows of exile and displacement Majumdar believed it produced for her mother, are at the heart of the story which the *Family History* tells, making it as much Hemangini's story as it is Janaki's. Indeed, although the history of Janaki's husband opens the book and that of W.C.'s political career frames the major arcs of the narrative, it is the drama of a daughter striving to understand her mother's life and preserve it for posterity that ultimately makes the *Family History* what it is: a memorial to a certain kind of Indian nationalist heroine.

The original manuscript, which is written in Majumdar's hand and which runs to over 200 pages, opens by evoking the village community in which her husband, Prio Krishnar Majumdar (1879–1947), was born and raised.[2] The Majumdars were *zamindars* in the vicinity of Murshidabad, and orthodox Hindus. But P.M. (as Janaki refers to him throughout the manuscript) was not destined to follow in the family footsteps.[3] Not only did he pursue a career in engineering and the law, he 'lost his faith in the gods' as a result of a childhood incident and became a 'rationalist'—a path toward unbelief (if not secularism) which was uncannily matched by his future father-in-law's rejection of religious orthodoxy of all kinds. Like W.C., P.M. too was educated in England, and the tales of his time in London and Birmingham as a student add ethnographic depth to recent historical scholarship about the experience of Indians in Britain in the nineteenth and twentieth centuries, especially where social life is concerned.[4] As Rozina Visram has suggested, by the First World War there was a considerable Indian population in Britain, located mostly in metropolitan areas and comprising students, businessmen, parliamentarians, and revolutionaries.[5] This 'community in the making', as Visram calls it, was a highly mobile one: not only did students pass through and return again in later life as professionals or tourists, they often used Britain as a base from which to pursue careers in other outposts of empire. Like Mohandas K. Gandhi a generation before, P.M.'s career took him to South Africa and eventually to Calcutta, where he worked at the High Court. The Bonnerjee family's migrations from Calcutta to London and back again were certainly not representative of most Indians' experiences in the pre-war period, but they were quite typical of a pattern of elite male mobility dating from the 1860s— mobility linked inextricably to the quest for professional credentials, civil service certification, and political influence with the imperial government at Westminster.

The fact that Majumdar begins the *Family History* with P.M.'s genealogy and delays discussion of the Bonnerjees' story until Part II reminds us that her chief audience for the manuscript was not 'the public' but her children and grandchildren—the extended Majumdar/Bonnerjee clan rather than the Bonnerjees per se. It also tells us something about the challenges she faced as she tried to balance her account of W.C.'s very public career with the narratives of domestic culture to which she devotes so much attention in the text. W.C. Bonnerjee was a larger-than-life figure whose early law career and later political accomplishments inevitably dominated Bonnerjee family lore. His illustrious Brahmin pedigree, his early academic successes, his role not just in founding the INC but in establishing a network of politically-minded diasporic Indians in Britain from the 1860s onward—all of these distinctions made him the most celebrated Indian nationalist of his day. One contemporary observer remarked that he cut a very fine public figure, 'with a handsome face, and a graceful flowing beard ... suave manners ... and ... an almost musical tone in his rich voice'.[6] In the words of one of the first historians of the Indian National Congress, Bonnerjee was prime among 'our Indian Patriarchs'.[7] This is not to suggest that his was the only form of nationalist politics on offer in the late nineteenth century, nor that within INC circles his reform programmes went unchallenged, whether by 'extremists' or 'moderates'. B.G. Tilak and G.K. Gokhale had very different relationships with the imperial state and, for that matter, saw themselves as representing different 'indigenous' communities than Bonnerjee or the early INC.[8] There were, moreover, differences and rivalries that dated from the very founding moments of the Congress itself, despite the hagiographical air with which he tends to be treated in biographical accounts, and despite the fact that the 'growth of national feeling and unity of Indians' was what Bonnerjee hoped the INC would accomplish.[9] W.C. was, for his part, among the most anglicized in the first generation of nationalists, a feature of his public persona which helped to secure his place as a venerable political leader, and not just for English observers. As the Special Correspondent for *Reis and Rayyet* wrote in his sketch of the first meeting of the INC in 1885, 'his dress was English, his every attitude, sitting or standing was English, from a gentle wave of his hand to a slight toss of the head, he looked, in fact, every inch an Englishman'.[10]

Significantly, that same correspondent concluded by saying that, 'for all that' W.C. 'looked every inch a Hindoo'.[11] Reconciling those two identities was a struggle for many England-returned Indians of W.C.'s generation who came back full of admiration for English habits and ways of life. In Janaki's estimation, this was her father's story. As she recalled half a century later, he had made many friends in England and was deeply impressed by English freedom. He liked the English manner of living, and became a keen politician and an ardent feminist, and resolved never to go back to Hindu ways, but to bring his wife out of purdah and if he had children to give them all education on English lines, and in England if he could ever afford it.

'Going native' in this context meant developing not just an aesthetic appreciation for English customs, but a critique of Hindu and Christian orthodoxies as well. According to her account, he was greatly influenced by the atheism of Charles Bradlaugh and Annie Besant; though Besant's free-thinking had not yet extended to India, Bradlaugh was deeply involved in Indian nationalist activities in Britain.[12] Though Majumdar makes no reference to it, W.C.'s experience in London as a twenty-year old law student was fraught with temptation: temptation for alcohol, for meat and to surrender to the solicitations of English women as well. Only a decade or so after Janaki's *Family History* was penned, W.C.'s cousin Manickal Mukherjee published a book of letters written by Bonnerjee from London to his family in India which revealed at least one dalliance with a Miss Winter, who allegedly proposed marriage.[13] Such entanglements were by no means uncommon among Indian men educated in England during in the 1860s, 1870s and 1880s, as Gandhi's own autobiography, *My Experiments with Truth*, testifies.[14] These sexual encounters were complicated by the fact that most Indian men travelling to Britain for study were already married, often to child-brides who they left at home. This was certainly the case with W.C. Bonnerjee, who had married Hemangini before he want to Britain—a fact which helps explain the pathos with which Janaki treats Hemangini and her marriage from the moment it enters the narrative of *Family History*.

As I have argued elsewhere in more detail, Hemangini is arguably the sainted centre of *Family History*.[15] Her early life and marriage get some more attention than W.C.'s, and the sacrifices she made so that he could go to Britain are quite heart-breaking: not only did he leave her behind with his family, but he effectively out-casted them both by crossing *Kalapani* (Black Water). Though it is difficult to reconstruct the precise chronology of events from Majumdar's narrative, it seems possible, if not likely, that Bonnerjee encouraged Hemangini to explore Christianity once they were living in London so that she could find community of some kind and mitigate the trauma of living as an outcaste woman doubly burdened by the difficulties of exile. Janaki's sister Nellie Blair recalled that 'as far as I remember Papa wished her to become a Christian. He thought it would be easier for her when she had to live in England'.[16] Majumdar writes that 'she joined the Plymouth Brethren and became a firm and a devoted adherent to this sect'.[17] In any case, it is clear that for Janaki, the combination of W.C.'s English-inspired aspirations—political and cultural—and her mother's relatively uneducated, orthodox background meant that Hemangini's life as a wife and mother was difficult, painful, and with few rewards save the joy of her children. To be sure, Majumdar repeatedly assures her readers that Hemangini was a good, kind, patient, and forbearing woman; a woman who loved her husband and strove to accommodate his desires and satisfy his determination to live life 'in the English style': a woman who found tremendous solace in religion and was both respectable and respected in the various communities in which she found herself. And yet, as Majumdar's description of Bonnerjee family life in Calcutta and especially suburban London suggests, the changes—in household routine, architectural layout, and the gendered geography of domestic space—which W.C. enacted in the name of reform made Hemangini uneasy, especially because they drew her into more of a public role than she might have desired. Or at least, so her daughter tells us. Again, Majumdar insists that her mother was good at all the things W.C. Bonnerjee asked of her: she could manage servants, navigate the London shopping scene, and even cope with the opening up of her house every Sunday to all manner of Indian students and visitors who, evidently, she fed and watered on a regular basis. Despite the trauma of exile, the challenges of conversion, and the experiences of English racism which her children endured—and, of course, because of them—Hemangini emerges in *Family History* as a kind of martyr-heroine, not just of Bonnerjee family life but of the first decades of Indian nationalism as well.

Students of Indian nationalism, and especially of the historiographical debates which have surrounded the question of the relationship of women and gender to nationalist rhetoric and practice in nineteenth and twentieth century India, will find in Hemangini an especially interesting historical figure. *Family History* represents her first as a devout Brahmin girl and wife, then as an equally devout Christian convert. Such postures were profoundly at odds with her husband's secular beliefs, and this contrast allows us to appreciate in new and perhaps more nuanced ways the dichotomy of home-as-spiritual-domain, world-as-political-domain that Partha Chatterjee and Dipesh Chakrabarty have both suggested structured Indian nationalist (and especially Bengali) cultural life.[18] There have been numerous critical elaborations of this reading by scholars using evidence from a variety of archival sources in the service of an equally various set of historical and political questions.[19] Hemangini's story as represented in *Family History* bears out these critiques, insofar as it testifies to the powerful and often coercive geographies, especially of reformed domestic spaces, as well as to the ways in which women were capable—whether intentionally or not—of enacting a kind of conservative modernity in response to the pressures of elite male nationalist reform projects. To put it simply: at least in part because her husband wished it, Hemangini helped to promote a 'progressive' Indian nationalist agenda by virtue of the kind of family life she oversaw and the kind of house she kept.[20] Like many modern women and even some feminists, she drew the domestic into the gaze of the public, thereby politicizing it in new though culturally quite familiar ways.[21] In many ways, the version of Hemangini which *Family History* offers flies in the face of such binaries as public/private and inside/out and illustrates—quietly, subtly, but in the end, quite persuasively—that the domestic is always already the public, the private is always already the national, and the household is always already the political.

Because *Family History* is a memoir as well as a domestic chronicle, it could be argued that what Majumdar remembers and records here tells us a lot about its author and little or nothing about the 'real' Hemangini. To some extent, this is true. Hemangini left no letters or diaries that we know of, though *Family History* and Mukherjee's book both indicate that she wrote to W.C. while he was studying in Britain and kept a regular housekeeping journal.[22] In terms of accessing her historical experience, however, we have to rely largely on what we know from Majumdar's account, which paints her sympathetically but also relentlessly as a figure of 'simple shrewdness'. The comparative hollowness of Hemangini's subjectivity raises questions about the limits of our historical knowledge not just of Indian women, but of all those who have left few written traces or none at all. Rather than dwelling on whether or not Hemangini felt the way her daughter says she did, it is more instructive perhaps to reflect on what Majumdar's account of her mother tells us about *her* subjectivity—especially when we remember that Janaki and her brothers and sisters were similarly, as well as differently, the objects of W.C. Bonnerjee's reform agendas. Born a year after her father was elected president of the INC for the first time, Majumdar spent most of her childhood in London.[23] She went to school in Croydon, where the Bonnerjees had a house; and she eventually matriculated at Newnham College, Cambridge, thereby helping to fulfill her father's aspiration that his daughters have only the best that British education had to offer. According to a correspondent to the London *Times*, at the time of Majumdar's death in 1963, she was the first Indian woman to receive a degree in Natural Sciences—and she also had a 'thorough knowledge of English poetry'.[24] Majumdar was in many respects the embodiment of the modern progressive woman—a twentieth century version of the 'New Woman' in whose image W.C. had tried to fashion Hemangini through contemporary models of household management and domestic engineering in the house in Croydon in the 1870s and 1880s. If Majumdar objected to her own education or was uneasy about it in any way, these ambivalences do not register directly in *Family History*. But we might read her determination to rescue her mother from the recesses of nationalist history—to excavate Hemangini's story as the foundation of Indian nationalism as her father envisioned it for Indian families and, by extension, Indian society—as a critique of the costs of his modernizing mission. In this sense, *Family History* does some of the same ideological work which feminist historians of India have recently tried to do with respect to the question of 'the Indian woman': that is, it makes clear the extent to which her emergence in history has been treated as an emblem in the service of both nationalist and colonialist patriarchies.[25]

There were Indian women in Majumdar's time who were actively engaged in a multi-pronged anti-patriarchal critique. Pandita Ramabai (1858–1922) and Rukhmabai (1864–1955), both of whom came of age a generation earlier than Majumdar, erupted into the imperial public sphere in the 1880s as contentious female/feminist figures who took aim at indigenous male orthodoxy and the colonizing projects of the masculinist imperial state.[26] Ramabai especially lived large in twentieth century public discourse; when she died in 1922 she was mourned by the *Times of India* as one of 'makers of modern India'.[27] The decade in which Majumdar wrote *Family History* was, admittedly, a very different political moment, especially for 'the woman question'. Far from being resolved by emergent and competing nationalist discourses, the 'problem' of Indian women and their role in anti-colonial movements was very much open to debate—as the lingering effects of the *Mother India* controversy set in motion by Katherine Mayo in the late 1920s testifies.[28] Whether Majumdar found company with these earlier women, and how or whether she responded to the Mayo debates or contemporary Gandhian agitation by women, is difficult to know with any degree of certainty. I feel confident in saying that she did not intend the writing of *Family History* as an overtly political act, at least not at a conscious level— even though she makes reference to Gandhian activity of her time (via the participation of one of P.M.'s relatives in non-cooperation) and was conscious of the fact that she was committing the Bonnerjee/Majumdar tale to paper fifty years after her father's INC triumphs.

On the other hand, it is possible to read Majumdar's text as an implicit engagement with events of the time, even if we can only speculate about its significance for inter-war Indian politics on a world stage. What does it mean, for example, to recapture the silent, respectable, domesticated heroism of a Victorian woman for Indian nationalism at a historical moment (the mid 1930s) when Indian women were erupting into public spaces as part of the anti-colonial struggle, chanting *Bande Mataram*, as many did in the wake of Gandhi's salt marches and *satyagraha*?[29] What might it mean for the daughter of a prominent Indian nationalist to document the fundamentally transnational character of the first stage of Indian nationalism during a time when the claims to the nation-ness of India and to the representativeness of Congress were not just being contested but ridiculed and reviled by British officials and in the metropolitan press?[30] What does it mean when a person of Majumdar's background and connections does so with the intention of keeping private the stories she tells—that is, not in circulation or for public consumption? And what can it mean that this chronicle of a prominent and very public family should scarcely allude to worldly events—save those related to the INC—that are absolutely crucial for understanding W.C. Bonnerjee in context, or for sign-posting major events like the World Wars? These are some of the questions raised by *Family History* and its intersection with nationalist and feminist histories.

In this sense, Majumdar's *Family History* has something in common with another text recently brought to our attention by a feminist historian: Tanika Sarkar's edited volume *Words to Win*, which reprints the first autobiography written by a Bengali woman, *Amar Jiban* by Rassundari Devi (1876).[31] If the other-worldliness of that text is historically intelligible—it is very much a piece of devotional literature, quite enclosed in the space of hearth and home, written by someone who did not travel abroad and was focused on her role as a good Brahman woman—this point of similarity raises interesting questions about the relationship between the public and private, the personal and political, in Indian women's writings during an extended historical moment, which might look quite fractured to us (the 1870s versus the 1930s), but which may be of a piece if we imagine different periodizations than those conjured by the descriptors 'Victorian' or 'late-colonial'. With respect to the question of privacy versus publicity, it should be noted that Majumdar collaborated with Sadhona Bonnerjee (a grandchild of W.C.) on a short pamphlet called *W.C. Bonnerjee and Hemangini*, published by Janasiksha Prochar Kendra (Calcutta, *c* 1975). This is a highly hybrid text, drawing on extracts from a volume published by Sadhona in 1944, on the centenary of W.C.'s birth, and on parts of Janaki's *Family History*, in some places more or less verbatim.[32] Significantly, and in contrast to the *Family History* manuscript, *W.C. Bonnerjee and Hemangini* privileges W.C.'s public career, narrating in encyclopedic detail his early training, his rise to political prominence, and his various achievements in the field of nationalist politics. The section on Hemangini comprises only about a fifth of the slender pamphlet; what is not lifted directly from the *Family History* text is overlaid with political commentary, thus effectively diminishing Hemangini's role, especially in contrast to the centrality of her story in the manuscript drafted by Majumdar. Also, since

W.C. Bonnerjee and Hemangini was published over a decade after her death, it is not clear what, if any, role Janaki had in shaping the pamphlet, or in integrating sections of her *Family History* into it.

There is no reason to suppose that Majumdar would have objected to such a project. Indeed, it is quite likely that she would have seen it as a fitting tribute to her mother, and of a piece with her own determination to set the record straight when it came to Hemangini's role in shaping the kind of Indian nationalism W.C. stood for (though whether she would have approved of her being so subordinate to W.C. is another matter). Majumdar wrote another memoir/history which was also to see the light of day posthumously. This one was called *Pramila: A Memoir*, and was devoted to the life of her sister, nicknamed Milly. It too bears some of the traces of the 'original' *Family History*, though the story cleaves much more closely to Milly's life than to family life; and the editor, Muchu Chaudhuri, Milly's son, indicates that the published version (issued in London, sometime in the 1970s) may have been edited significantly. It also has dense footnotes, apparently written by Chaudhuri, which do more than supplement the text. Through these, he has ended up writing a contrapuntal memoir of his own, pinning his own memories of his grandmother, the houses she lived in, and the glimpses of Bonnerjee family life he was able to recapture to the dominant narrative Janaki establishes. In the process, he marks out a series of generational differences, of perspective and affect. In the preface to *Pramila*, Chaudhuri declares that he is grateful to his aunt (whom he refers to as Agnes, not Janaki) for having created a life-story for his mother, though he remarks with some astonishment on its insular character and its relative isolation from world events. Significantly, one of the anecdotes from *Family History* which does not make it into *Pramila* is the one about Indian Sunday dinners at 'Kidderpore Croydon', as the Bonnerjee manse in suburban London was called. Chaudhuri laments the lack of attention to culinary detail in his preface because he wanted to know what they ate not just on Sundays but every day as they tried to recreate India in Britain. The aroma of 'a real, authentic Indian meal'—so evocatively recalled in *Family History*—is what he finds regrettably missing in *Pramila*. What did his forbears do, he wants to know, 'in those days, [when] every other London street didn't have a restaurant serving curry as it does now[?]'[33]

For all its attention to genealogical facts, *Family History* is, in contrast with *Pramila* and in absolute terms, full of the rich detail of the everyday, culinary or otherwise. Majumdar has as much of an eye for drama as she does for detail. The pathos of her mother's exile is matched by the evocative accounts of the voyage to Britain, house life in both Kidderpores, school culture in Croydon, and the terror of local racism at the hands of their English landlords, the Woods. Equally visible is the world of middle-class prosperity and privilege within which the Bonnerjees lived their peripatetic family life. Servants are ever-present but chiefly as backdrop, even as the challenges of managing a transnational corps of domestic workers is woven into the story of Hemangini's household successes. To be sure, Janaki seems driven at moments by an inexorably chronological impulse; significantly, most dates are linked to familial events or conjugal choices, making this a 'family' history in form and content, routine and rhythm. But her ethnographic eye, articulated through memories of the material spaces of home, evidences an architectural imagination which is extremely compelling. Her talent for ethnography includes a recognition of the need for 'native informants', as the insertion of testimonials from her sister Nellie Blair and others demonstrates. All of these elements make *Family History* more than simply a history: it is, both literally and figuratively, an archive of the domestic culture of late Victorian Indian nationalism in diasporic form. Readers of the text may find themselves frustrated by how delayed Majumdar's own story is, how deeply embedded the arc of her own narrative is, how elusive her 'self' is in the work as a whole. Even when we get to Part III ('Early Married Life'), we relive the death of Hemangini which has already been rehearsed in some detail, and then we move quickly to the birth of Majumdar's daughter, and then back to the details of her siblings' lives, careers, and children. If Hemangini is the saintly centre of the memoir, her very centrality tends to prevent a space for Majumdar, or at least to preclude the possibility that she is to be found here—except, of course, as she is refracted through her mother's experiences, both 'domestic' in the private sense and historical in the public sense. The homes which Majumdar recreates in such detail in the course of her narrative, also compete with her as the protagonist of this story, signalling as they do the impermanence of some interiorities, and the ghostly traces they leave *in* and *for* history.

In fact, so powerful were the images of house and home which structure *Family History* that they have made their way into contemporary Bonnerjee/Majumdar memory in poignant and telling ways. The wife of Majumdar's grandson Amar, Sally Singh, recalled in 1996 that when Amar's sister visited the last family house ('Point Clear' in Darjeeling) 'she was so disappointed with the old house about which she had heard so much'. According to Sally, even after Majumdar went to live in London (where she was to die) to be with her children and grandchildren, the spectre of the family's former homes continued to haunt the family imagination:

> throughout this period and of course ever since, the family's identity was very closely tied to the house in Darjeeling ... some of its best furniture came from the house in Calcutta, then was shipped to London. The reconstruction of the family again took place through the memories of that house. I think it was very necessary for them to have this 'created' base as almost all the descendants ended up in England, Canada and the States where they were unknowns. No one recognized them as descendants of W. C. Bonnerjee, they were just 'Indians'.[34]

Whether all the Bonnerjee descendants shared or continue to share this status anxiety, is impossible to know.[35] The long reach of house-life, with all its material and immaterial influences, is nonetheless remarkable, and not merely because it persisted across considerable time and space, at least on Janaki's side:

> Besides the family memoirs [Sally continued], there was also a great emphasis on speaking English 'correctly'. I would almost say that there is a 'Bonnerjee' accent which is quite recognizable. The women in the family who wear saris also drape them in a way that I have never seen outside the family. Another feature that always amazed me was that most members until recently fed their children the diet that Victorian nannies thought was good for children, so no rice and curry until they were almost adults. These were just a few of the most noticeable traits that have survived their colonialist heritage.[36]

If the servants are relatively invisible in *Family History*, the impact of the nannies, at least, has been enduring. Such continuities are undoubtedly aided by the reproduction of the elite lifestyle W.C. and Hemangini together fashioned for their large family across several generations, and by the patrimony, both material and metaphoric, which W.C. bequeathed them. If *Family History* is a private family heirloom as well as a now-public archive, it has survived precisely because it is a product of the privileged diasporic circuitry which is such a crucial part of the Bonnerjees' historical legacy.

There is much more to be said about this document. The spirituality and religiosity it evokes; the dense histories of family life, sibling affection, and parental anguish it records; the upward mobility, failed careers, disappointments, and materialist aspirations it chronicles—all these narratives, and more, await analysis by students of nationalist, feminist, and postcolonial India. Meanwhile, the publication of Majumdar's *Family History* follows a tradition in Indian feminist historiography of bringing the lives of women to the sightline of contemporary readers. Geraldine Forbes' pioneering work with the autobiographies of Shudha Majumdar and Manmohini Zutshi Sahgal has been carried forward by Tanika Sarkar's aforementioned *Words to Win*—which is, in turn, part of a self-consciously named 'archive series' published by the Delhi-based feminist press, Kali for Women.[37] Susie Tharu and K. Lalita's two-volume *Women Writing in India* is literally a treasure trove of material dating from 600 BC to the present, and is especially valuable because it gathers, annotates, and historicizes fragments as well as pieces of longer texts.[38] More recently, the memoir of a contemporary of Majumdar's, Cornelia Sorabji, has been re-issued by Oxford University Press under its original title, *India Calling*.[39] The sheer density of archival evidence now available 'in public' speaks to the promise of Indian women's history in the twenty-first century, both as a practice of recovery and as a site of resistance to and critique of dominant narratives, nationalist and otherwise. More work needs to be done to problematize the elitism of the voices we have, and to excavate and re-materialize traditions of speech and work and practice that fall outside now-canonical spheres—whether those spheres are regional, cultural, religious, or political. Interrogating the 'politics of difference' in Indian women's and feminist history, which have arisen even and especially among progressive scholars is crucial to this project, as Rajeswari Sunder Rajan's and Anupama Rao's critiques of brahmanical feminism have consistently reminded us.⁴⁰ Only then can the historical significance of an artifact like Janaki Majumdar's *Family History*—which, for all its cosmopolitanism, is rooted in such specific caste and class locations—be fully appreciated.

December 2002　　　　　　　　　　　　　　　　　　　　　　　　A.B.

Notes

¹Mrinalini Sinha, 'The Lineage of the "Indian" Modern: Rhetoric, Agency, and the Sarda Act in Late Colonial India,' in Antoinette Burton, ed., *Gender, Sexuality and Colonial Modernities* (London: Routledge, 1999), pp. 207–21. See also Partha Chatterjee, 'The Nationalist Resolution of the Woman Question,' in Kumkum Sangari and Sudesh Vaid, eds, *Recasting Women: Essays in Colonial History* (Delhi: Kali for Women, 1989, pp. 233–53); Dipesh Chakrabarty, 'The Difference-Deferral of (A) Colonial Modernity: Public Debates on Domesticity in British Bengal,' *History Workshop Journal* 36 (1993): 1–33; Sonia Amin, 'Childhood and Role Models in the Andar Mahal: Muslim Women in the Private Sphere in Colonial Bengal,' in Kumari Jayawardena and Malathi de Alwis, eds, *Embodied Violence: Communalising Women's Sexuality in South Asia* (London: Zed Books, 1996), pp. 71–8; and Himani Bannerjee, 'Fashioning a Self: Gender, Class and Moral Education for and by Women in Colonial Bengal,' in Kate Rousmanière et al., eds, *Discipline, Moral Regulation and Schooling: A Social History* (New York: Garland, 1997), pp. 183–218.

²For a contemporary comparison see Nilmani Mukherkee, ed., *A Bengal Zamindar: Jaykrishna Mukherjee of Uttarpara and His Times, 1808–1888* (Calcutta: Firma K.L. Mukhopadhyay, 1975).

³Hindu wives, especially upper-caste ones, were not to refer to their husbands by their given name. Thanks to Geraldine Forbes for clarifying this for me.

⁴*Ayahs, Lascars and Princes: The Story of Indians in Britain, 1700–1947* (London: Pluto, 1986); Antoinette Burton, *At the Heart of the Empire: Indians and the Colonial Encounter in Late-Victorian Britain* (Berkeley: University of California Press, 1998); Shompa Lahiri, *Indians in Britain: Anglo-Indian Encounters, Race and Identity, 1880–1930* (London: Frank Cass, 2000); Rozina Visram, *Asians in Britain: 400 Years of History* (London: Pluto, 2002).

⁵Visram, *Asians in Britain*, pp. 44–104.

⁶*Reis and Rayyet*, quoted in Iqbal Singh, *Indian National Congress: A Reconstruction, v. 1 1885–1918* (New Delhi: Nehru Memorial Museum and Library, 1988), p. 12.

⁷This is Pattabhi Sitaramayya, quoted in Singh, *Indian National Congress*, p. 12.

⁸For a variety of perspectives on this phenomenon see Stanley Wolpert, *Tilak and Gokhale: Revolution and Reform in the Making of Modern India* (Berkeley: University of California Press, 1962); Hira Lal Singh, *Problems and Policies of the British in India, 1885–1898* (New York: Asia Publishing House, 1963); Anil Seal, *The Emergence of Indian Nationalism: Competition and Collaboration in the Later Nineteenth Century* (Cambridge: Cambridge University Press, 1968); Jim Masselos, *Towards Nationalism: Group Affiliations and the Politics of Public Associations in Nineteenth Century Western India* (Bombay: Popular Prakashan, 1974); Sumit Sarkar, *Modern India, 1885–1947* (New Delhi: Macmillan, 1983); Richard Sisson and Stanley Wolpert, eds, *Congress and Indian Nationalism: The Pre-Independence Phase* (Berkeley: University of California Press, 1988); and Sanjay Seth, 'Rewriting Histories of Nationalism: The Politics of "Moderate Nationalism" in India, 1870–1905,' in *American Historical Review* 104, 1 (February 1999): 95–116.

⁹Singh, *Indian National Congress*, pp. 1–20; quote is p. 21.

¹⁰Quoted in Singh, *Indian National Congress*, pp. 12–13.

¹¹*Ibid.*, p. 13.

¹²See Sadhona Bonnerjee, *Life of W.C. Bonnerjee, First President of the Indian National Congress* (Calcutta, n.d. [c. 1944]).

¹³Manicklal Mukherjee, *W.C. Bonnerjee: Snapshots from his Life and Letters* (Calcutta: Deshbandu Book Depot, 1949), p. 18.

¹⁴Mohandas K. Gandhi, *An Autobiography; or the Story of My Experiments with Truth* ([1927] Reprint: Ahmedabad: Navajivan Publishing House, 1990). For more detailed accounts of Indian travelers in Victorian Britain see Burton, *At the Heart of the Empire*, ch. 1, 'The Voyage In'; and Visram, *Asians in Britain*, chs 3 and 4.

¹⁵Antoinette Burton, *Dwelling in the Archive: Women Writing House, Home and History in Late-Colonial India* (New York: Oxford University Press, 2003), ch. 2, 'House, Daughter, Nation: Interiority, Architecture and Historical Imagination in Janaki Majumdar's "Family History"'.

¹⁶See *Family History*, 2.4.

¹⁷See *Family History*, 2.12.

[18]Chatterjee, 'The Nationalist Resolution of the Woman Question', pp. 233–53, and Chakrabarty most recently in *Provincializing Europe: Postcolonial Thought and Historical Difference* (Princeton University Press, 2000), ch. 8.

[19]See for instance Kamala Visweswaran, 'Small Speeches, Subaltern Gender: Nationalist Ideology and its Historiography,' in Shahid Amin and Dipesh Chakrabarty, eds, *Subaltern Studies IX* (Delhi: Oxford University Press, 1996), pp. 83–125; Judith Walsh, 'What Women Learned When Men Gave Them Advice: Re-writing Patriarchy in Late-Nineteenth Century Bengal,' in *Journal of Asian Studies* 56, 3 (1997): 641–77; and Himani Banerjee, Shahrzad Mojab and Judith Whitehead, eds, *Of Property and Propriety: The Role of Gender and Class in Imperialism and Nationalism* (Toronto: University of Toronto Press, 2001), to give just two examples.

[20]For two accounts of the stakes of this project for Bengali nationalist ideology see Judith Walsh, 'The Virtuous Wife and the Well-Ordered Home: The Reconceptuialization of Bengali Women and their Worlds,' in Rajat Kanta Ray, ed., *Mind, Body and Society: Life and Mentality in Colonial Bengal* (Calcutta: Oxford University Press, 1995), pp. 331–363; and Pradip Kumar Bose, 'Sons of the Nation: Child Rearing in the New Family,' in Partha Chatterjee, ed., *Texts of Power: Emerging Disciplines in Colonial Bengal* (Minneapolis: University of Minnesota Press, 1995), pp. 118–44.

[21]This was by no means unique to Indian women in India; see Leonore Davidoff and Catherine Hall, *Family Fortunes* (University of Chicago Press, 1987) and Antoinette Burton, *Burdens of History: British Feminists, Indian Women and Imperial Culture, 1865–1915* (University of North Carolina Press, 1994).

[22]Mukherjee, *W.C. Bonnerjee*, p. 25.

[23]He was elected to a second term in 1892.

[24]'Mrs Agnes Majumdar,' London *Times*, 10 June 1963, p. 23. Thanks to Kate Bullard for this reference.

[25]Lata Mani, *Contentious Traditions: The Debate on Sati in Colonial India* (Berkeley: University of California, 1998); Mrinalini Sinha, 'Refashioning Mother India: Feminism and Nationalism in Late-Colonial India,' in *Feminist Studies* 28, 3 (Fall 2000): 623–44; and Tanika Sarkar, *Hindu Wife, Hindu Nation: Community, Religion and Cultural Nationalism* (Delhi: Permanent Black, 2001).

[26]For Ramabai see Meera Kosambi, 'The Meeting of the Twain: The Cultural Confrontation of Three Women in Nineteenth Century Maharashtra,' in *Indian Journal of Gender Studies* 1, 1 (1994): 1–22; Kosambi, ed., *Pandita Ramabai Through Her Own Words—Selected Works* (Delhi: Oxford University Press, 2000); Inderpal Grewal, *Home and Harem: Nation, Gender, Empire and the Cultures of Travel* (Durham: Duke University Press, 1996); Uma Chakravarti, *Rewriting*

History: The Life and Times of Pandita Ramabai (New Delhi: Kali for Women, 1998). For Rukhmabai see Sudhir Chandra, *Enslaved Daughters: Colonialism, Law and Women's Rights* (Delhi: Oxford University Press, 1998) and Antoinette Burton, 'From Child Bride to "Hindoo Lady": Rukhmabai and the Debate on Sexual Respectability in Imperial Britain,' in *American Historical Review* 103, 4 (1998): 1119–46.

[27]Quoted in A.B. Shah, ed., *The Letters and Correspondence of Pandita Ramabai* (Bombay: Maharashtra State Board for Literature an Culture, 1977), p. ix.

[28]See Mrinalini Sinha, ed., *Mother India* (Delhi: Kali for Women 1998; Ann Arbor: University of Michigan Press, 2000).

[29]Geraldine Forbes, 'Goddesses or Rebels? The Women Revolutionaries of Bengal,' in *The Oracle* 11, 2 (April 1980): 1–15; Visweswaran, 'Small Speeches, Subaltern Gender,' pp. 83–125; Uma Rao, 'Women in the Frontline: The Case of U.P.,' in Leela Kasturi and Vina Mazumdar, eds, *Women and Indian Nationalism* (New Delhi: Vikas, 1994), pp. 28–52. For an account of pre-Gandhian women's agitation see Bharati Ray, 'Calcutta Women in the Swadeshi Movement (1903–1910): The Nature and Implications of Participation,' in Pradip Sinha, ed., *The Urban Experience: Calcutta* (Calcutta: Riddhi, 1987), pp. 168–81.

[30]W.H. Morris-Jones, '"If It Be Real, What Does It Mean?": Some British Perceptions of the Indian National Congress,' in Sisson and Wolpert, eds, *Congress and Indian Nationalism*, pp. 90–120.

[31]Tanika Sarkar, *Words to Win: The Making of Amar Jiban: A Modern Autobiography* (New Delhi: Kali for Women, 1999). For a comprehensive overview of Indian women's writing see Susie Tharu and K. Lalita, eds, *Women Writing in India: 600 BC to the Present*, vols 1 and 2 (New York: The Feminist Press, 1991). For histories of Indian women see Radha Kumar, *The History of Doing* (London: Verso, 1994) and Geraldine Forbes, *The New Cambridge History of India: Women in Modern India* (Cambridge: Cambridge University Press, 1996).

[32]See Bonnerjee, *The Life of W.C. Bonnerjee*.

[33]Agnes Janaki Penelope Majumdar, *Pramila: A Memoir* (London: Contemprint Ltd., n.d.), p. 2.

[34]Sally Singh to the author, 21 November 1996.

[35]Milly's son Muchu claimed she had not such sentimentality about the Croydon house, and that she never took him to see it when they traveled to Britain together in the 1920s. See Majumdar, *Pramila*, p. 3.

[36] Sally Singh to the author, 21 November 1996.

[37] Geraldine Forbes, ed., *Memoirs of an Indian Woman* by Shudha Mazumdar (New York: M.E. Sharpe, 1989); Forbes, ed., *An Indian Freedom Fighter Recalls Her Life* by Manmohini Zutshi Saghal (New York: M.E. Sharpe, 1994); see also Forbes and Tapan Raychaudhuri, eds, *From Child Widow to Lady Doctor: The Memoirs of Dr. Haimabati Sen* (New Delhi: Roli Books, 2000).

[38] Tharu and Lalita, eds, *Women Writing in India: 600 BC to the Present*, vols 1 and 2.

[39] Chandani Lokugé, ed., *India Calling: The Memories of Cornelia Sorabji, India's First Woman Barrister* (Delhi: Oxford University Press, 2001).

[40] Rajeswari Sunder Rajan, ed., *Signposts: Gender Issues in Post-Independence India* (New Delhi: Kali for Women, 1999); and Anupama Rao, ed., *Caste, Gender and Indian Feminism* (forthcoming, Kali for Women). I am grateful to Anu Rao for sharing the draft of her introductory essay for this volume with me.

Family History

The following is an attempt to jot down the main facts of the family history of both the Majumdar and Bonnerjee families, so that our children and great grandchildren may not be entirely ignorant of the history of their forbears. No apology is required for making this attempt; so many changes have taken place and are still taking place in India and the whole world since the time when this family history begins, with the birth of my father-in-law in 1822, that it becomes almost a duty to try to look back at things as they were then, while records are still available, and people still alive who can remember the past.

—Janaki Agnes Penelope Majumdar

Part 1

The Majumdar Family

1.1

P.M.'s Ancestry

My husband's father, Gopi Mohun Majumdar, was born in the year 1822, son of [a] *zamindar* of Islampur in the district of Murshidabad—long before the Mutiny, in the reign of George IV when Queen Victoria was only three years old. Murshidabad being one of the stronghold of the Mogul influence, Gopi Mohun was much impressed by Persian ways and manners, and used to dress his children in Persian costume. The Islampur house was built by his ancestor Jonardhan, who was the actual founder of the present family; but Gopi Mohun, who was a strong man and a good administrator, added on to and improved the house, and worked up the *zamindary* from more or less insignificance to wealth and importance. As well as practically rebuilding the family house, he established a school and a dispensary, dug tanks, and planted trees. A full account of his doings and the history of his ancestors, who trace their descent to the Sen kings of Bengal who ruled in the 12th century, will be found in the large red book entitled *History of Murshidabad* by Major Walsh.[1]

Gopi Mohun married as his third wife,—the other two having died childless, and very young,—Gopesweri, the daughter of a family living in the village of Goash of the same district. She married before she was ten years old, and history relates that her eldest child—a girl, Modan Mohini—was born when she was only eleven years old. She had in all twelve children of whom ten—three sons and seven daughters—lived to grow up and many have children of their own. She died at the age of eighty-four in the year 1924—hale and hearty to the last, with all her senses unimpaired—as the result of a fall and fracture of the thigh bone. Her's was a very gentle and beautiful nature, calm and placid. Her children relate that they never once saw her lose her temper, and she was invariably kind and considerate to everybody—deserving or undeserving. Her husband's sisters lived in the house and managed all the affairs and brought up the children, so Gopesweri's life was mainly concerned with having the children, and performing all possible religious ceremonies for their health and safety. My husband Prio Krishnar was her eleventh child, born on 2 February 1879 at Islampur. He was rather delicate in his infancy, and owing to a severe illness, was dedicated to Haridas, and in the family he was and is still known by that name.

Village life then was very much the same as it now, only there was less malaria and people were altogether healthier and better off. The Majumdar family were highly orthodox Baishnabs, belonging to the Vaid caste; and the main events were the different seasons of the agricultural year and the Pujah festivals. His father died when P.M. was only five years old, and the estate was managed by the eldest son Rai Bahadur Hari Krishna (18?–1896).

1.2

Early Days

In the Murshidabad district there were many English indigo plantations, and Babu Hari Krishna as well as his younger brother Charu Krishna (1864–1908) became friendly with some of these and with other English settlers, so that the Persian influence was gradually replaced by English influence upon the menfolk of the family. The women remained then, as they still do, entirely orthodox Hindus. The men took to riding and shooting and pig-sticking and polo with their English friends, and used to entertain and be entertained by them. They rented a house in Berhampore, the nearest town at a distance of 16 miles from the village of Islampur. The road was only a 'cutcha'[2] one, and there were the rivers to cross; and to cover the distance between Berhampore and Islampur one had a choice of the following conveyances—*palkies*, relays of ponies, elephants or bullock carts. Later on, one could drive half way in a ticca garry[3]; and now one can go the whole way in a motor car! I have tried all these conveyances at one time or another, and can definitely say that the last is the best!

The brothers would spend a good part of the year at Berhampore, and took up various public works—District Board Membership, Honorary Magistracy, etc. They used to spend money very freely and give loans to planters and others, and although they both became Rai Bahadurs[4], a drain began on the estate from which it has never recovered.

P.M.[5] went to school at Islampur and took from there, at the age of thirteen, his entrance examination or Matriculation as it was then called. His chief friends were the sons of two of his sisters, Nalini and Bidya— the sisters being so much older than himself that their children were his contemporaries. My father-in-law followed the old plan adopted by some *zamindars*, of marrying his daughter to *ghur jamais*—i.e., making the son-in-law live in his village, instead of sending the daughter to her husband's home. He built houses near the big house for the daughters and their husbands and gave them presents of land. P.M.'s chief friends were Nalini Das Gupta, his eldest sister's third son, and Bidya Jyotish Chundar Roy, the eldest son of his third sister, both of whom were about his age. The three boys went to school and played together. They well remember their first visit to the town of Berhampur which seemed to them a most marvellous place; with great joy they sniffed the wonderful 'town-smell' not realizing it was chiefly drains! They drank with awe and wonder their first bottle of lemonade which cost them five annas and considered it a terrible waste of money. It was many years before they saw a train, and one of them was considered rather a hero because he had once passed near a station, and although no train was in sight, he reported that he had seen the smoke left behind by a train that had just gone.

P.M. was always passionately fond of games of all kinds, and also of horses. His early recollections are of creeping out of the house unobserved in the hottest part of the day, catching horses grazing in the fields and riding bare-backed, with a strip of rope for reins. Another favorite pastime was to bribe the syces[6] of planters stabling their horses at the Islampur house-stables for dak[7], with saris stolen from his mother's box, and taking the horses out for a gallop, unknown to the owners. Mr William Moray, an Irishman, initiated him and ... in the sport of pig-sticking in the Panchananpur jungles. This was a truly delightful sport, and he has never forgotten the thrill when he was taken to his first meet at the age of twelve or thirteen. He was lent a mount and spear, and in due course a pig broke out and was given chase ... . Experienced pig-stickers avoided the water and took a circuitous route, but he ... took a short cut ... and was nearly drowned!

At that time there was an indigo planter named McDonald who used to keep a big stable and drive a tandem, with a hunting horn to disperse traffic. P.M., one day, took it into his head to emulate this turn out. He got hold of two unknown tats,[8] rigged up a harness with bits of rope and string and put them in a trap tandem fashion; and with a number of chokras[9] to help him, drove in great style along the Goash road, with a tin cannister to be beaten instead of a horn. One of the chokras was running beside the leader to keep him in the way he should go, but when this lad's attention was momentarily distracted the leader decided to turn round, hoping to graze in a ditch near by. To avoid a catastrophe, the wheeler was also turned and eventually the leader, wheeler, trap, chokras, and driver, all landed in a melée in the ditch. However, no bones were broken and they managed to sort themselves out and get home safely.

One of P.M.'s worst crimes in his childhood was disappearing for a whole day. It was Pujah time and his brothers had presented him with a beautiful velvet suit trimmed with gold braid and a new pair of shoes, too small for him, which he wore all night, having been told they would grow! Having exhibited the costume to his friends at home, he decided to go and show it to a school friend who lived some distance away, and never thought of telling anyone where he was going. He slipped into the stable and bribed the syce to let him have a large horse and somehow managed to get away without being seen. Once out of sight, he began to enjoy himself, got safely to his friend's house, and there, had a large meal and plenty of fun. Some tenants, on seeing him, presented him with 'Nazar'.[10] When he was coming home at sunset, he met some servants hunting for him, who told him his eldest brother had set out search parties in all directions, and that he might expect a good beating when he got home. Such an end to this day of pleasure had never been expected by him, and he began to feel distinctively uncomfortable. However, he managed to creep into the inner apartments unobserved, and by remaining there for some days managed to avoid the well-deserved beating by clinging to his younger sister-in-law's anchal,[11] as his eldest brother could not come where she was!

1.3

Religious Influences

As has already been said, the Majumdar family were devout orthodox Hindus, and both men and women kept up all the usual observances. P.M. was brought up in this atmosphere, and the first stories he heard were tales of the gods and goddesses, told to him by the womenfolk and also by the old servant Kailash, who is still at Islampur. He declares now that during a thunderstorm he always remembers Kailash's explanation of the lightning as a fairy running away from the pursuit of the thunder god who roared with vexation as she escaped. After a bad dream, he was taught to write 'Ram Ram Ram' on his pillow with his finger, and this always prevented further nightmares that night. He took his Sacred Thread at the age of ____[12] with other cousins and nephews of the same age, and took it all very seriously. He was taught to revere Brahmins, especially the priestly family or Thakurs at Islampur, though he never liked the young men of that family. One of the reasons for this was sheer misunderstanding. He was driving along one day in his pony-trap, very proud of being out alone, and in all friendliness waved his whip at Jotin Thakur. Unfortunately the tip of the whip cord touched Jotin Thakur and he went home livid with fury complaining that the *Chok Babu*[13] had whipped him, and P.M. got the worst punishment of his life without (for once!) deserving any.

The way in which he lost his faith in the gods was a curious one. The headmaster of the school, a Brahmin, used to come at mid-day everyday to the Islampur house to rest in the *baithakkhana*,[14] as it was the only place in the village where there was a fan. He used to frequently ask for a glass of water or for some sweets from the inner apartments. Now to get these was a long hot walk, and as P.M. was the youngest member of the family, the duty usually devolved upon him, and very unwillingly he had to get up and fetch the requisitioned refreshments. He had been taught that any, even the slightest, token of disrespect to a Brahmin would be visited by an instantaneous punishment from the gods. One day, while fetching some water, and because he was very thirsty, he took a sip out of the glass and waited, secretly terrified, to see how he would be punished. Nothing happened. A few days later he went so far as to lick a piece of the *shondesh*.[15] Again, nothing happened. He then decided that if he was not punished for two such gross pieces of wickedness and disrespect to a revered Brahmin, then there was no god. After that, all religious observances became meaningless to him. Not only that, but in later life he came actually to hate the idols for being the means by which poor people's superstitions were worked upon; and to dislike all priests of whatever religion for playing upon human weakness for their own profit. For those who were themselves dupes, he was very sorry; but for those who knew what they were doing and yet continued their 'priestcraft' as a means of self-advancement, he has the severest condemnation. He gradually came to a rationalistic outlook, where he refused to believe anything on hearsay to which his reason would not assent; while agreeing that there must be a Force beyond the universe which brought it into being and keeps it going, he holds that there is no proof that this Force is in any way concerned with individual human beings.

1.4

College Days
Calcutta and Creek Row

After passing the Entrance Examination, P.M. was sent to the Berhampore College, but after a short while there, it was decided that he had better go to St. Xavier's College, Calcutta, and arrangements were made for him to join the Hindu hostel in 1893. Always of an independent nature, he decided when he got to Calcutta that he would not go to the hostel, but arranged to board with an Anglo-Indian master at St. Xavier's called McGrath who lived in Ripon Street. This was his first experience of really living in English style, and he liked it very much indeed, and found the Anglo-Indians whom he met very interesting and entertaining. In fact it became the summit of his ambition to live in Creek Row among the flower of Anglo-India!

In those days, Anglo-Indians thoroughly despised 'natives' as a class, though they were friendly enough to those whom they thought had money and position. But if a 'native' wanted to be on good terms with Anglo-Indians he had to be careful to be very English in his ways, and it was fatal to wrap up his school lunch in Bengali newspapers, or put much oil on his hair!

The Jesuit Fathers did splendid educational work among the Bengalis and Anglo-Indians then, as now. It was at St. Xavier's College that P.M.'s friendship with N.C. Mallik began, and that friendship has continued up to this day. N.C. Mallik's father, Hem Chandra Mallik, was a very well-to-do gentleman from a good Kayastha family, and although himself an orthodox Hindu, he liked to meet Bengalis on a grand scale in his beautiful house at 12 Wellington Square. N.C.M. was an only son, but his cousin Subodh (father's brother's son) whose parents died early, lived with Mr H.C. Mallik. Subodh Babu afterwards took a great interest in politics and was one of the first Bengalis to be sentenced to deportation for his political opinions.[16] He was the idol of the earliest Swaraj party and called Raja Mallik, who by degrees gave all his money for political purposes, selling his share of no. 12 to N.C.M. He died in Darjeeling in 1920, a comparatively poor man.

1.5
First Marriage to Wife's Death
1894–1899

P.M. was married in an orthodox Hindu fashion—and with great ceremony to Prativa, a daughter of Babu Moti Lal Sen, cousin of the famous Keshub Chunder Sen.[17] In a box at Islampur is still carefully preserved his wedding dress of green velvet and gold braid, along with the wonderful dresses his brothers wore when they were made Rai Bahadur. There were all sorts of ceremonies and feasting when Prativa came to Islampur, but unfortunately their happiness was short-lived as—always delicate—she developed phthisis[18] and died shortly after her first baby was born, the baby girl dying too.

This connection brought P.M. many new friends, as the Sens were a clannish family, and Keshub Chunder Sen's children adopted him as a brother, as did Keshub Chunder Sen's brother's family—Krishto Behary Sen's children. Shortly after his marriage he began going to Lily cottage, and tells many stories of the glory of Keshub Babu's eldest daughter Sunity[19]—the Maharani of Cooch Behar—and her brothers Nirmal and Peter who were respectively her Military Secretary and Private Secretary, and the third daughter Sucharu who married the Maharaja of Mourbhurg. Of course these bright stars were far too grand for him to become familiar with, besides being much older, but he used to go to play with the younger brothers, Saral (Bhopal) and Bhajan and so saw something of their grandeur, and they were all exceedingly kind to him. P.M. was one of the first to possess a bicycle, of the penny farthing type, and used to ride on it and pretend to be able to do all sorts of trick riding, which sometimes came off and sometimes did not!

1.6

Work at Gidhaur
1900–4

From the year 1892 Babu Charu Krishna had been working as Manager of the Tikari Estate at Gaya, as his brother was managing the Islampur Estates which did not require two people to supervise it. But in 1896 Babu Hari Krishna died very suddenly from an attack of apoplexy, at Berhampore, which was of course a terrible grief to the whole family. Charu Babu then took over the management of the Islampur property. After the death of his wife P.M. was very much upset and unsettled and decided to take some job elsewhere, and managed to get the post of manager to the Maharaja of Gidhaur, in Bihar. Here he worked for nearly four years and thoroughly enjoyed being 'on his own' and acquired a vast deal of ... management [experience] in the care and breeding of horses, entertaining the Maharaja's guests of all nationalities, distinguished and humble, and the art of living alone. He had quarters at Gidhaur and also a bungalow at a place called Chakai not very far from Simultala which was then under the auspices of Sir Tarak Nath Palit, B.L. Gupta, Sir R.N. Mookerjee and Lord Sinha[20]—(all then plain 'Mr')—fast becoming a distinguished health resort. Here he became acquainted with all these people and their families, many members of which he vastly admired in all simplicity, because they were 'England returned'. Here also he had his first experience of champagne dinners, at the first of which he failed to get drunk in spite of a great effort, but felt so exceedingly uncomfortable that he has never been able to like champagne since then. At Chakai he grew friendly with the Mission Doctor and his wife whom he sincerely admired and who helped him during his various ailments, polo accidents and such contretemps.... Living alone made him a great newspaper reader, and from that time till now he is never happy unless he has read at least one newspaper from end to end.

It was with the Maharaja of Gidhaur that P.M. attended the first great Durbar at Delhi organized by Lord Curzon. This was a marvellous pageant held in 1902 for ... King Edward's Coronation. The Gidhaur party were in tents, and how bitterly cold it was under canvas in Delhi, only those who have been to Delhi in winter can realize. He was amused at the procedure of ceremonial visiting by the Maharajas at that time. He would perhaps accompany the Maharaja on a state call upon some other Maharajas. Upon arrival, greetings were exchanged, then both Maharajas and their suites would sit in complete silence for ten minutes or so, after which the visiting Maharaja would rise and take his leave. Later in the day, the other Maharaja would come to return the call in exactly the same fashion.

In Gidhaur, P.M. used to discuss spiritualism and supernatural phenomena with some of the Maharaja's relatives, and especially with one of his uncles, but they could never come to any definite conclusions. This uncle made a pact with P.M. that whoever died first would come and tell the other if there is any life after death, or any way by which the spirit world can manifest itself. A short while after this the Uncle died, and P.M., though secretly terrified, was determined to go through with it, and sat for hours by the dead body waiting for some manifestation, which never came neither then nor afterward.

On the Maharaja's lands in Behar, mica abounds, and P.M. became very much interested in schemes for mining this mica and making a commercial success of it. While his ideas were materializing, a Government Scholarship was offered and advertised in the papers—for students wishing to take up a course in mining engineering at Birmingham University. The course was a three year one, and £200 a year was the amount of the scholarship. P.M. put in an application for this scholarship and was lucky enough to obtain it. He therefore hastily wound up his affairs at Gidhaur, and without waiting for the consent or otherwise of his relatives, started off for Bombay where he caught the P&O mail steamer 'Victoria' for London.

1.7

Student Days in England
1904–7

P.M. now confesses that he did not much enjoy the voyage in a small cabin shared with another Indian student, and that he felt seasick off and on. This seasickness began soon after leaving Bombay because he had to completely unpack his biggest box in a rough sea to get out the matches he had put at the bottom, finding from a printed notice that it was strictly prohibited to carry matches in boxes in the hold! However, after three weeks of discomfort through rough seas, and lack of exercise, he got safely to London. There he was met at the terminus by Mr Mohi Mohun Ghose (Ling) who was our connection by marriage, as he had married, in succession, two of Mr K.B. Sen's daughters who were cousins of P.M.'s first wife (Mr K.B. Sen was a brother of Keshub Chunder Sen). Ling Ghose's first wife was a beautiful creature who died young leaving two sons, Gita and Tutu. He afterwards married her sister, but there was rather a sad little scandal about that marriage, as apparently the girl was found to be pregnant just after marriage, and Ling never forgave the deception. She died, I fancy, when the baby was born, which also died, so the pathetic little incident was wiped out. Ling was in the Indian Civil Service, and a brilliantly clever man, but unfortunately he took to drink which ruined his career. Much later he married Ida Dutt—of whom more will appear in this record—and had another son, Joy, who unfortunately is not right in his head, and though in his twenty-sixth year, is like a child and can do nothing for himself.

Whatever may have been Ling's faults, P.M. says he will always be extremely grateful to him for his kindness in meeting and looking after him a shy young student. He really did his best for him 'after his fashion', by taking him with him to bars and saloons and trying to show him something of the world! Luckily P.M. had been cured of all desire to drink after his Simultala experience, and had a strong head—otherwise one trembles to think what might have happened to him under such guidance! He learnt to be very clever at pretending to drink without really doing so, and quietly disposing of his glass of whiskey in some convenient receptacle. There was an historic plant in Ling's room which anticipated Sir J.C. Bose's experiments on plant-stimulation by alcohol by dying from overdoses of whiskey!

However, P.M. was not long in London, as his course of study was at Birmingham University where he took a degree in mining engineering. As the engineering college was not residential, the students used to stay in a hostel with students of other colleges, the bulk of whom were theological students. As has been related, P.M. had already lost his faith in Hindu priests, and he says that from watching these theological students he very soon lost his faith in Christian seminarists too!

1.8

Friends and Acquaintances

As his scholarship was a small one, and he did not want to ask for money from home, he used to eke out his allowance by coaching other students, especially a Chinese student who needed help. P.M. also decided to take his Bar examination at the same time, in order to have two strings in his bow. This necessitated periodical visits to London for examinations and dinners, and when there he used to stay at a boarding house in Addison Road kept by a Miss Dutt—the Ida Dutt aforesaid—to which he was recommended by Ling Ghose.

Ida's father was an Indian doctor settled in England who had married an Englishwoman. Their's was a family of five daughters and one son. The son, Newton Dutt, first had a job in Messrs Dent and Co., publishers, and later on got the post of Librarian to the Maharaja of Baroda's State Library where he spent many happy years. He is an exceedingly nice man and perfect brother, and has remained a bachelor all his life. He is afflicted with a cleft palate, but in spite of his disability has always made good. Dr Dutt died leaving his family very badly off, so the daughters tried in turn to earn their own livings. The eldest, Mabel, who was born in the late sixties, went as housekeeper-companion to Mrs Palit (later Lady Palit, wife of Sir Tara Nath, a very rich and peculiar man) and afterwards married her son Loken Palit who was in the I.C.S. Ida kept a boarding house for Indian students, and it was here that P. M. found himself on his visits to London. The next sister, Leila, was and is still eccentric and has had to spend various periods in mental homes. Rena, the next one, married a Mr Khan of the Indian Medical Service, and the youngest, Muriel, looked after the mother so long as she lived and then came to help Ida with Joy. Now, they are all widows and are living in the two houses in Golders Green which Loken left to Mabel Palit on his death.

Mabel and Ida are both the kindest of women, but Ida was almost too kind as a boarding house keeper, and being slightly eccentric and not at all a good manager, she could never make both ends meet, nor make the house comfortable or attractive ... . At Ida's boarding-house P.M. also met three young girls who came as 'Lady Helps'—Mary Barnes who was very pretty and attractive, tall and slender, and who had stage ambitions and managed to get taken on as a chorus girl for short periods: she subsequently married Kabla Sen; Violet Sandbach, a clergyman's daughter, who married Harry Sen, son of Mr P.C. Sen of Rangoon; and 'Baby', who married Sitish Chakravarti.[21]

P.M.'s chief friend at this time was an Assamese man, R.N. Chaudhury, who was well-to-do and had a motor car which P.M. used to drive for him as he himself could not learn to drive, and they had many pleasant excursions in this car—and a few accidents! There were very few cars in those days, and taxis were only just beginning and were called 'taximetre cabs', so there was a certain cachet in possessing and driving a car, and P.M. greatly enjoyed it.

In Birmingham, P.M. made several friends and used to spend weekends with the families of his fellow-students, and play a lot of hockey in the winter. He also took up boxing with an instructor and went to a good many dances. He felt the cold very much, chiefly because he did not take any precautions against it, though he must take a cold bath every day, and never having heard of hot-water bottles, was tortured by cold feet at night as well as a chapped body from the ice cold water! These were the sacrifices he paid the gods of hardiness and hygiene!

After three crowded years in England, he successfully passed his engineering examinations and also his Bar examination, was duly called to the Bar, and succeeded in getting a very good post as Manager to a Diamond Mine in South Africa at Cronstadt on a contract, with passage paid both ways. This was a triumphant end to his student career, and he started off on a Union Castle liner for Cape Town, accompanied by one of the Directors of the Mine with high hopes of a successful career.

1.9

Experiences in South Africa

These hopes, however, were not destined to be fulfilled. Neither he, nor the directors, had realized the strength of feeling in South Africa against Indians, and it was a shock of surprise to realise from the boat onwards how far 'colour prejudice' could go. Upon landing at Cape Town, he found he could no longer be classed with 'white' people—only certain hotels would harbour him, and there he must have all his meals in his bed-room, he could not travel in ordinary trains or trams. In short, he found he must submit to being treated as an ordinary coolie. Mr Gandhi, then a barrister practising in South Africa, found himself under the same disabilities, and began his fight against oppression, and championship of the oppressed. But nearly 30 years after these events the position is still the same, although the Government of India deplores the state of affairs and has appointed an Indian Commissioner to do what he can. So far nothing has been done, and Indians in South Africa are treated in exactly the same way as they were in 1908.

After trying hard for some months to settle down and make the best of it and get on with his job, P.M. found it was hopeless to do anything under these conditions, and laid his case before the directors. They could not but realise the truth of his statements, and after some delays, agreed to pay him a lumpsum as compensation, and pay his passage back to India, an offer P.M. was glad to accept.

In spite of all this, he found his time in South Africa intensely interesting, and visited various towns including Johannesburg. Individual Boers and English settlers were often very kind and friendly, and he met some very nice people there. But he was not at all sorry to depart, and sailed on the Union Castle Liner ... to Durban and from there through Zanzibar to Bombay by a German boat.

1.10

Return to India
1908

When P.M. got back to Calcutta, he found that his brother was in very bad health and had gone to Allahabad for treatment. He accordingly repaired thither, and found Charu Babu very unwell, in the hands of a Yogi who was treating him for asthma and other complications, and held out high hopes of recovery, which alas! were not fulfilled. From Allahabad—where his sudden and unexpected arrival was a great joy to all the family and especially his brother—they went to ... Barrackpore, still searching for health. But in spite of a great number of doctors and a variety of treatments nothing could be done, and to the great grief of all the family Charu Babu died a few months after his brother's return.

An account of the surviving members of the Majumdar family would not be out of place here. That is to say, as they were in 1908, for many have died since then.

The eldest brother Hari Krishna Majumdar was married when he was very young, to an orthodox village Hindu girl, also extremely young. She must have been a pretty child, as she still, at the age of well over seventy, has a lovely face and features, the great charm of which is due to their sweet expression. At the beginning of their married life they had several sickly infants who died shortly after birth—and then in 1884 [came] a son, Tryambal Krishna, who was a fine healthy infant; and there were great rejoicings at his birth. After him, two daughters and two sons lived to grow up. The eldest son was always called Tom, and the eldest daughter Lily (*b*. 1886), the other girl Gati (*b*. 1888) and the two boys Pranavar Krishna (Pinu, *b*. 1890) and Probor Krishna (Piboo, *b*. 1893).

Charu Babu was married to a sister of the famous chemists of Colutala, C.K. Sen and Co., and she created a great sensation when she came as a bride to Islampur, as she was the only Calcutta member of the family and was considered extremely fashionable! As well as the one sari worn by the other women and girls at that time, she wore an undergarment, and even a blouse, and when her babies came along, they used to wear real baby clothes which had never been seen before. P.M. was very fond of both his sisters-in-law, and the younger one became a great companion. When in Calcutta, he used to see a good deal of her brothers and nephews and nieces, many of whom became lifelong friends. The workings of their large business which included, as well as the running of the shop, Kaviraji treatments from a resident doctor and the management of a newspaper 'Hitabadi', were of perpetual interest and educating to P.M. and he was initiated into all the intricacies of advertising and propaganda which were a great surprise to him. The Sen family were—and are—very well-to-do and most of their money has been made from a patent hair-oil called 'Jabakusum Tel' which sold then and still sells like hot cakes. I was amused, when I was in Calcutta, to hear one of the grand-daughters affirm that neither she nor any of her relatives ever used Jabakusum oil, because not only did it not do any good to one's hair but it caused bald patches!

Charu Babu and his wife had five children, one son and four daughters. Sidhu, the only son, was at this time a student in Calcutta together with Pinu and Piboo, working for I.A. and matric respectively.[22] The eldest daughter Pravabati, always called Heli (from Helen!), was just married to Dr Aprakash Sen (Ram) of Delhi son of Babu Sansar Sen, Dewan of Jaipur State; and Lily was also married to Nibaren, a nephew of the same family, whose father was Principal of the Jaipur School of Art. Heli has always been prosperous and happy with her husband and two sons, Nikhil and Anil. Dr Sen is a very well-known and highly respected doctor at Delhi and the sons have done well, one in [the employ of] Reuters, and the other is now (1935) a medical student in Bombay. Lily's husband unfortunately proved to have no money-making capacity, and they have just managed to struggle on in Calcutta. She had four sons and three daughters, but one son was drowned while bathing in 1930 ... and one daughter (Dhebi) died of phthisis. The eldest son, Bhutan, is doing well in the Geological Survey of India; and the twins, Gour and Nitai are still students. The other two girls, Baby and Sankori, are happily married with several children each. But this is anticipating.

Of Charu Babu's other daughters, the second, Puti (Daritri), was just married at this time to Keshub Chunder Gupta, a police court pleader, and the two others were then about 10 and 11 and unmarried. Raju married Paresh Gupta, a pleader, in 1919 and Radha married Nirmal Gupta who had a job in the post office.

After Charu Babu's death, P.M. decided to start practice in Calcutta, and established himself in a flat at 98 Dhurrumtollah with Sidhu, Pinu and Piboo and Raju and Radha, leaving Tom to look after the Islampur Estate. Tom had lately married Panchanani, daughter of A.C. Sen, a Delhi Bengali—related to Sansar Babu—in charge of a printing press at Delhi.

1.11

Work in Calcutta

Accordingly, P.M. was enrolled as a member of the Calcutta Bar and began working at the High Court. He bought a high trap and a pony for evening drives, although he used to go to court on a bicycle at that time. He was glad to meet his old friend N.C. Mallik again, and also Mrode's (Omy's) cousin Satyen Mallik, whose father Nogen Mallik had just built a palatial house called 'The Minar' in Lower Circular Road, very near P.M.'s flat. He used to go there often, as well as to 12 Wellington Square, and also had many other friends in Calcutta. Lily's husband's family house was very near, and also Puti's family house was within easy reach, so the boys and girls were catered for in their leisure time; and of course Sidhu's uncle's families at Colutala were at hand, as well as other relations.

At this time P.M. was very friendly with Sir Tarak Nath Palit and his daughter Lil, and it was mainly through them that my husband and I eventually met.

Sir Tarak Nath Palit was a very wealthy eccentric and quarrelsome man, who had been to England and liked the life there so much that he had his son and daughter educated there, just as my father did. My father was a close friend of Sir Tarak Nath Palit, and one of the few with whom he never succeeded in quarreling. They had been fellow students in London in the sixties. Sir Tarak Nath had three sons and one daughter. With his eldest son he quarrrelled, and drove him out of the house because he wanted to marry an English girl and they were never reconciled in spite of all the efforts of their friends. Lady Palit was a quiet self-effacing little woman who was terrified of her husband and obliged to do whatever he ordered her, though they quarrelled perpetually. Loken was a very fine, intelligent, cultured man who passed into the Indian Civil Service, and married Mabel Dutt as has been already described. He and his father were never on very good terms. The next brother, Shatu, was also a very fine man and got on with both parents, but unfortunately he died in his early manhood. The father was very fond of his only daughter Lil, who was, and still is, a woman of exceptional culture, genius, and charm, but—as could only be expected in such a family—she was wild and flighty, made an unhappy marriage, and afterwards left her husband (Sisir Mullick) and son for another man with whom she seems at last to be happy. Her career caused great excitement in the Calcutta of 1909, as such things as divorce were scarcely ever heard of in those days! Lil was always a great friend of my sister Milly in their girlhood, and even in those early days her escapades and affairs used to astonish us.

As has been said, P.M. became very friendly with this family at that time. Sir Tarak Nath took a great fancy to him and used to make him come almost every day and drive his car, to teach his Chauffeur. Through the Palits he met the Sinha family, Mr S.P. Sinha being then at the top of his form and in high favour both with the government and the Congress Party. He had begun life in quite a humble way, and after he was called to the Bar, did so badly for nearly 10 years that he was thinking of trying to get a munsiffship[23] somewhere. At that time his luck began to turn and he began making a lot money, and was appointed first Standing Council, then Advocate General, and finally Law Member to the Government of India. He was knighted and later became Lord Sinha, was given a seat in the House of Lords, became Under-Secretary for India under the Montague-Chelmsford regime and was later appointed Governor of Behar. Here he was thoroughly unhappy, his health broke down completely and his family caused him a lot of worry as all his three daughters turned out unsatisfactory—of whom more mention will be made later. To make a long story short, he eventually died a broken-hearted, disappointed, unhealthy man in 1928, to whom a magnificent and unique career, unheard-of honours and riches beyond the dreams of avarice could not bring happiness.

1.12

Sisters and Relatives

At this point I propose to write a short account of P.M.'s sisters and their families, as that has not yet been done. As has already been noted, his father wanted to have his daughters near him, and chose for some of them husbands who would be willing to settle down in the village of Islampur, for whom he built small houses near the big house. The eldest daughter, Modan Mohini was married to Babu Rajendra Das Gupta, and her house is very close to the big house. Her husband ... was a very nice man who acted for some time as Postmaster at Islampur. They had five sons and two daughters: Sri Mohun and Saroj Mohun, who were a few years older than P.M.; Nalini Mohun, about his age and playfellow at school; Haripada (Mohini Mohun) and Ram; and the daughters, Suroma and Santi, who married very young and scarcely ever came back to Islampur. Sri Mohun and Saroj Mohun were fine, clever boys and after taking their B.A. examination one became a Deputy Magistrate ... . In 1913 a most terrible tragedy occurred. Saroj was taken ill with small-pox, Sri Mohun went to nurse him and caught it and they both died. Nalini, who has a job with C.K. Sen and Co., also went, caught the disease, but recovered. Sri Mohun's first wife had died and he married again, a niece of Banshi Dhar Gupta of Chapra, and had two sons, Kalipada and Rash Behary, and three daughters—all married now—Annapurna, Narayani, and Sivarani. Saroj, also a widower, married Banshi Babu's daughter and had six children, and their story is almost t[ragic]: [after the] father died, the eldest son Satyendra died of typhoid, and another child also died of the same disease. A few years after that, yet another child died, and some years after, one of the two surviving daughters, who was just married to a suitable young husband, died in childbirth, the baby dying too. There are now only two surviving children, a son, Buro, and a daughter, Manik, who is married and has children of her own, her husband being a son of the Guptas of Panchanput near Islampur. In spite of all these disasters, Saroj Mohun's wife never complains nor bewails her hard lot, and though quite heartbroken regards it as *kopal*—i.e., her fate. She has never had any psychic experiences, but her sister-in-law and cousin, Indu, Sri Mohun's wife, has had several strange experiences which are worth recording. I am told that she was a nervous and rather hysterical girl who, when first married, used to have a species of fits. These were put down to a sort of 'possession' by the first wife, through jealousy of her successor! She completely got over these attacks and was a very happy wife and mother, touring with her husband wherever he was stationed. After his death, she had two very strange visions. When Satyendra was ill with typhoid, her son Kalipada was also dangerously ill, and she was completely worn out with nursing him. One night, she told me, she was watching him alone when she saw her husband come into the room. She was quite calm, and oddly enough his presence seemed perfectly natural. He told her that the boy would recover, from next day the fever would begin to go down, and there was no need for further anxiety. As she was so exhausted, he told her, he had been allowed to come and help her, and he urged her to lie down and sleep a little while he watched. She was so convinced of his presence and of what he said, that she allowed herself to be persuaded to lie down and immediately fell asleep. Towards dawn, she felt him waken her and tell her he must go, and she got up soothed and refreshed and resumed her watch. The next day, the fever began to go down and all went well. She told me this story only a year or two after the incident, and was still absolutely sure that Sri Mohun really had been with her.

The next incident was this. She was very anxious to arrange for Narayani's marriage, and the people who were helping her told her that the choice lay between two young men, A and B (I cannot remember their names). Both seemed equally suitable, and when Narayani was taken to be inspected by their families, both parties were agreeable. It was therefore left to Indu (Narayani's mother) to decide which young man to select for her son-in-law. While she was worrying about this, she told me her husband came to her in the early morning one day and said to her, 'Whatever you do, you must choose A for Narayani's husband. On no account choose B'. And without giving her any reasons, he disappeared. Accordingly, A was chosen and the marriage celebrated, and all has gone well. Six months after the wedding, news came that B had died suddenly of a snake bite.

I leave the reader to explain these incidents as he thinks best. They were related to me by Indu a year or two after they occurred.

To continue with the account of P.M.'s eldest sister's family, the other sons and daughters have all prospered with their families. Nalini married a sister of Mr S.K. Mallik, the Judge, and has three sons and two daughters (Rothin, Tunu, and Kabul, and Asha and Ranu, all married except Kabul). Haripada, who is a doctor, married Nonilata daughter of Babu B.C. Sen of Hazaribagh, and has four daughters and two sons; One daughter, Mitu, is deaf and dumb (poor child!) and is at the Deaf and Dumb School in Calcutta. Ram married a relative of the C.K. Sens. The two daughters married men in jobs at Rurki and Lucknow respectively.

P.M.'s second sister's husband, Krishna Ballabh Roy, was given a house and some lands about 15 minutes walk down from the big house, which—being in the open country—is always called 'Mather Bari' or Field House. This man was not so amenable as the other sons-in-law, but being of a very quarrelsome disposition quarreled with all the family in turn, gave his brothers-in-law and their sons endless trouble. His wife had 17 children, many of whom died very young. There was one son who lived to grow up, but he died also, long before his parents, and his death caused them great sorrow. Five daughters also lived to grow up, and marry, but as they were usually away at their husband's homes, the parents had a lonely life. The third sister and her husband died, leaving four sons .... The husband of the fifth sister as well as the girl herself also died young, and their son Phani died at the age of eleven or twelve. The sixth sister Anuj married Basanta Roy who was for many years head of the Cooch Behar State Treasury Office, and their children—Pachu, Jagadish (now dead), Arindam, and the daughter Bina who has also died—were born there. Both Anuj and her husband died very shortly after one another in 1918.

The youngest sister Chalu married Souribilash Gupta, a Deputy Magistrate and they had two sons and several daughters, and lived in a variety of districts. The eldest son, Potol, is in the Imperial Bank of India, stationed chiefly in the U.P. and the younger is struggling as a pleader in Burdwan. The daughters are married. Chalu died first a few years ago and Souribilash a couple of years later. As I write now, in 1935, the only surviving members out of all the twelve brothers and sisters are Biren's mother and my husband.

If Biren owes a debt of gratitude to P.M., so does Potol, because in the height of the Swaraj agitation in 1921 he was very anxious to become a professed follower of Mahatma Gandhi by non-co-operating, which would have meant giving up his work for the Intermediate Arts Examination, leaving College, and learning to spin, in the meantime giving up all hopes of a wage-earning career for some time to come. Being very torn in the mind, he wrote to his uncle asking his advice, and P.M. replied sympathizing with all his aspirations but at the same time strongly advising him to finish his college career before he came to any final decision about the future. This he did, and has never regretted it, when he sees how others of his contemporaries who 'came out' in the first flush of eager enthusiasm now swell the ranks of the unemployed. Mahatma Gandhi's ideas were sound, but unfortunately, the bulk of mankind being what it is, at that time little could be done by non-co-operating students [sic], though the spinning and Khadar campaign had a lasting effect on Manchester trade.

Having brought this history up to the point when P.M. first met his future wife, which actually happened at a tennis party at her house at 6 Park Street Calcutta, where he was brought by her brother R.C. Bonnerjee, a fellow barrister, in December 1908, I shall leave the fortunes of the Majumdar family for the present and give a brief account of the Bonnerjee family.

Part 2

The Bonnerjee Family

PART 2

The Bonnerjee Family

2.1

Ancestry of Womesh Chunder Bonnerjee

His Parents and Early Life, 1844–64

My father was born on 29 December 1844 at Sonai, Kidderpore, in the house of his grandfather Pitambur Bonnerjee. Pitambur was able to trace his origins to Pandit Bhattanarayan, one of the five Brahmins brought by Adisur from Kanauj in the middle of the eleventh century AD. The Bonnerjee family migrated to Baganda in the fourteenth century, and towards the end of the eighteenth century came to Calcutta, where Pitambur, who had been working as a schoolmaster, obtained a post in the solicitor's office.[24] Pitambur had three wives, eight sons and several daughters. His eldest son, Grees Chunder, my grandfather, became an attorney, and was one of the earliest Indian attorneys of the Calcutta High Court. One of his fellow clerks at that time was the father of Sir Charles Paul. One of my grandfather's brothers, Bhairub Chunder, became a *vakeel*[25] of the High Court, and some of the others worked as *muktears*,[26] revenue agents, etc.

Pitambur Bonnerjee was at one time a well to do man, with properties in Calcutta and Kidderpore, but he was inclined to be extravagant, not personally, but in performing expensive Pujahs and other ceremonies, and he gave away enormous sums in charity for both deserving and undeserving causes. His generosity to all who came to him became a family joke—no beggar was ever refused, and if there was no money in the house he would make his wives and daughters give up their jewellery. Things got to such a pitch that the ladies of the family were reduced to hiding away their valuable bangles and wearing brass ones about the house, or else their gold would be taken away to be given to some wholly undeserving beggar. Of course he always meant to give back in full measure what he had borrowed from them, being as generous to his own family as to outsiders, but it was not always possible to do this. The consequence of this was that he died a poor man, leaving his sons with heavy debts to tackle.

From Kidderpore, the family came to Calcutta and settled at Simla, at 69 Boloram De Street. Grees Chunder married twice, his first wife, Saraswati Debi, the mother of my father, being a great-great-granddaughter of the famous Sanskrit scholar Pandit Jaganath Tarkapanchanan of Tribeni in the district of Hughli. It was this famous scholar who was asked by the East India Company to codify Hindu Law to help English judges to administer it, and his code still survives as 'Jagannath's Digest of Hindu Law'. From this marriage were born four sons and four daughters, of whom Womesh Chunder was the second. The eldest son and the third son died as infants, so my father was virtually the eldest son; the other surviving son was Satya Dhone, who became an attorney. The four daughters were Mukhoda, Sukhoda, Patitpatani and Raj ... . By the other marriage there was only one daughter, Gonga Debi, who came in age between the second and third daughters of the other wife. The two co-wives were devoted to each other, and their children considered themselves one family. The second wife died young, but the other wife, my grandmother, lived to an old age, long surviving her husband.

My father was sent first to a *pathsala*[27] —where among his fellow pupils were Mr Nimai Bose, Abinash Chunder Ghose (afterwards Chief Interpreter of the High Court) and Khetter Mohun Ghose (Editor of the Lahore Tribune). He was then sent to learn English first at a Branch of the Oriental Seminary, and then at the Oriental Seminary itself, from where he was sent to the Hindu School. He afterwards confessed to having been an extremely lazy and unsatisfactory scholar and to having wasted his time deplorably at school, though he generally used to make up for it by brilliant examination results at the end of the term. He was very fond of amusing himself, and of going to the theater, and seeing he was not doing much good at school, his father decided to start him in a profession, and articled him to Mr W.P. Downing, an attorney of the

High Court in 1861. The following year he left Mr Downing, and became clerk to Mr F.W. Gillanders, and worked hard in this capacity for two years.

He used to tell us stories of his school days, of which I remember one, as a kind of ghost story. He was very friendly with one of the boys at the Hindu School, and one week-end this boy went to his village home. The night after he left, my father had to get up in the middle of the night, and as he was returning to his room, to his amazement he suddenly saw this school fellow standing in front of him. Before he could say a word the boy said, 'Moti (my father's nickname), I owe the school *durwan*[28] four annas[29] for tiffins[30] bought by him—please pay it back to him,' and disappeared. My father was utterly astounded, and though he hunted everywhere in that enormous house could find no trace of the boy. When he went back to the school on the Monday, eager for an explanation, he learnt that the boy had died of cholera the very night he saw him. This story was all the more astonishing to us, because my father disbelieved completely in ghosts, or any kind of supernatural phenomena ... .

At that time his father was not at all well off, and a wealthy marriage was arranged for him to my mother Hemangini, daughter of Babu Nil Money Motilal, an exceedingly well-to-do Brahman gentleman who owned most of Bowbazar. This was in the year 1859 when the bride was just ten years old.

2.2

Hemangini Bonnerjee
Her Parents, Early Life and Marriage
1849–59

Babu Nilmoney Motilal's first wife died, leaving one daughter, and he married a second time and had two sons, Nandagopal and Bujogopal, and one daughter, Hemangini. He was an exceedingly kind and generous man, and devoted to his youngest child, whom he used to take about with him wherever he possibly could contrive to smuggle her in. His wife was as strict and severe as he was easy and kind, and my mother used to confess how much afraid she was of her mother. The only time she softened was when any of the children were ill, and my mother told us that a timely head-ache was a great protection against her wrath. My mother was brought up as a strictly orthodox Hindu child and learnt to cook, but managed to pick up her letters from her elder brothers. She used to long to learn with them, and to go to school, and once tried to accomplish this by hiding under the seat of the carriage which took the boys to school, hoping that when they got there they would be bound to take her in to school too. Unfortunately she was discovered soon after starting, and ignominiously taken back and punished. One day, she was bathing in a tank under her father's auspices, and found she had lost irretrievably a silver chain she always wore. She was far too terrified to face her mother without it, so her father took her to buy another before they dared go home! He was very sorry to think of the fate that lay in store for her—early marriage, innumerable children, and hard work under a possibly cantakerous mother-in-law—so he tried to show her all he could of life in the ten short years of freedom. One day he took her to the house of a friend who sometimes followed English ways—one of the Tagore family, I fancy, so that she could see a dinner table laid in English fashion for a dinner party—a sight she would never see again, said he, thinking little of how she would one day be dining at Government House Calcutta!

Her great excitement used to be Pujah festivals and weddings. In those days there was no Hindu-Moslem problem, but Hindus would follow the Mohurrum procession beating their breasts, and Mahomedans would follow the Durga Puja procession. She told me she had been to so many weddings that when, at her own wedding, they called out 'Behold the bridegroom cometh,' she tried to run out with the other girls to have a look at him, quite forgetting that this was to be her own lord and master. He was much admired by all her relations for his good looks, and she was considered a lucky girl. When the bridegroom and the bride were left alone together for the first time, she told me the only remarks exchanged by them was her question as to how far it was from Bowbazar to Simla and his reply!

Shortly after her marriage she was sent to her father-in-law's house for a few months, and after that for ten years divided her time between the two houses. She was very happy at Simla House, and made what proved to be life-long friendships with all her sisters-in-law, and adored her brother-in-law Dhone, then a tiny baby. But she used to be very happy when the home carriage came to take her back to Bowbazar for a holiday; and proportionally sad when the Simla carriage called for her. Of her husband she saw very little for reasons to be explained in the next chapter. As has been said, her little brother-in-law Satya Dhone, who was then a small child, was devoted to her. In fact, she was the only person in the house whom he would obey at one time; before she went to her father's house she used to draw in chalk on the floor of her room the picture of an eye, and warn Dhone that although she herself was going away, her eye would be there to watch him, so he had better take care! I was reminded of this incident in Wiesbaden where the Greek Church has a painting of the Eye of God in the roof as a warning to worshippers to behave themselves!

My mother was a real saint, full of love for God and man, absolutely unselfish and uncomplaining, always kind and agreeable and the easiest person in the world to get on with. But she was no fool, and had a simple shrewdness of her own, and power of judging character. She was very competent in all household affairs and the management of servants, money, and had a keen sense of humor. She had a singularly upright nature, and was extremely tender-hearted and felt others' joys and sorrows as her own and was never jealous. She always deplored her lack of education, the fact that she never really learnt to speak English like an Englishwoman, though she began so young and had so much practice—and spelling was a perpetual bugbear to her! She was nervous and timid and very easily over-awed by her very assertive family, who perpetually domineered over her; and her husband was to her a real Thakur,[31] whose slightest wish must be carried out immediately. She was very shy and unready in society and very much afraid of people she considered superior in intellect to herself, and formal entertaining was a terror to her. But she had many devoted friends, and though her entire life was given up to serving her husband and children, she never forgot her friends. Her great support and refreshment was her religion, first as a devout Hindu, and later as a devout Christian.

At this time she was a very devout Hindu, careful and punctual in all observances, and was 'initiated'. At the initiation ceremony, the custom is for the priest to whisper in the ear of the person to be initiated a 'mantra' (holy sentence) which he or she must hear and remember and repeat daily throughout their life. If they cannot hear it when said by the priest, it cannot be repeated, and the ceremony is a failure, and the initiate boy or girl must go without a mantra. My mother, who was always very nervous and timid as has been said, often told me how terrified she was that she would not be able to hear her mantra, and that her very fear of not hearing would make her deaf, but luckily all went well.

She told me that in her youth she was hysterical, and sometimes used to suffer from regular fits during which she completely lost consciousness. At one time her elders decided that these fits must be due to possession by a devil, and accordingly an exorciser was summoned to drive away the devil; and this drastic treatment used to make her worse than ever. Once she was told, during treatment, to look into a certain mirror and report what she saw there, and to her horror she really saw the face of a terrifying old cook they used to employ, who had died years ago, with his head held at a characteristically crooked angle, as he used to carry it in life. This vision so frightened her that it took her hours to get over it then, and it remained an alarming memory throughout all her life. In later life she completely got over these hysterical affections.

She always told me she was an extremely plain child, with very projecting teeth; and that she grew up into a very plain young woman, as she suffered from leucoderma, which no treatment would cure.[32] But she must always have had lovely eyes and a sweet expression, and in later life, as I remember her best, the patchiness of her skin disappeared, leaving her really without the top skin, but the remaining skin was of a uniform white. Clothes held no interest whatsoever for her, and as soon as they were old enough, her children used to choose her dresses, but they could not prevent her from hiding her very shapely feet in large ugly shoes 'because they were comfortable'. At the time about which I am now writing, of course she wore only saris, and always went about bare foot.

2.3

W.C. Bonnerjee in England
1864–8

In the year 1864, when my father had been two years with Mr Gillanders, Mr Rustomji Jamsetji Jejeebhai of Bombay offered some scholarships to young Indian men to study law in England.[33] There were five scholarships in all, three to be given in Bombay, one in Bengal, and one in Madras; and in Bengal a committee was appointed to select a suitable candidate, the President being Mr Campbell (afterwards Sir George), a High Court Judge, and the numbers included two Indian gentlemen, Babu Prosonno Kumar Tagore and Nawab Amir Ali Khan. Out of about twelve candidates my father was chosen by this committee. But his father and all his relatives absolutely refused to give their consent to his going to England and thereby becoming an out-caste from orthodox Hinduism [sic]. They considered the whole idea absurd and the consequences of crossing Kalapani[34] unthinkable for an orthodox Brahmin, and told him to dismiss this ridiculous notion. When he found he had raised a hornet's nest about him, my father left home and spent a few days at his father-in-law's house in Bowbazar. From there, he went and saw a friend of his father's, Mr Cockerel Smith, attorney-at-law, who arranged for his going to England, and when all arrangements were made, my father secretly left the country.[35] His family knew nothing about it, and when he was found to be missing there was a tremendous disturbance and much lamentation for a long time. As soon as he got to England he wrote to his father who eventually forgave him and sent him some money, though strongly disapproving of his behavior. My mother told me she also came in for lot of abuse at that time and was called an unlucky girl and taunted with the fact that her husband ran away rather than have to live with her. Taunted for having no children.

My father was very happy in England.[36] Some other Indian men went to England in the same boat as my father. Mr B.L. Gupta passed into the Indian Civil Service and had a long and prosperous life, and became a life-long friend of my father, and even now his children are among our great friends. He never liked nor got on well with Mr Surendranath Banerjee.[37]

My father was very happy in England and in after life used to look back with pleasure on his student days. He joined the Middle Temple and worked extremely hard, both at law, and at perfecting himself in the English language. He learnt to speak beautiful and fluent English, and he told me that he did this by reading aloud to himself every evening when he first went to England. He was a great student and he studied at a great many other things besides law and began to take a great interest in politics. He was glad to break away completely from Hinduism, which had never had any appeal for him, and he was always very much against what he used to call 'priestcraft', meaning the methods by which priests of all religions are wont to prey upon the ignorance and superstition of the masses. He was very much impressed by the lectures of [Charles] Bradlaugh, whom he always considered a great hero, and he much admired Mrs Annie Besant.[38] He visited a great number of churches, and after told us that he was greatly impressed by Spurgeon's preaching, though he later became a bitter opponent of orthodox Christianity. His mind was that of a brilliant scholar and student, several decades ahead of his time, and he rejected Christianity as taught in the sixties, when the ... Bible was still considered to be an historical document, literally true from beginning to end for the following reasons: (1) He could not believe the Bible to be literally true, but considered the Old Testament as a collection of myths and legends put together by the Jewish priests after the captivity for their own purposes [sic]. This opinion was then considered wicked, immoral, and heretical, and yet we read in the 'New Commentary' issued by the S.P.C.K.[39] in 1928: 'Accustom your minds to regard Hebrew history as passing through the phases normal in all history—folklore, tradition, contemporary records, the free use of past history for purposes of present edification'—if only my father had been among people who could look upon the Bible in this way, he might have come to realize that 'it was to represent how a continuous purpose of God was at work in Israel .... It is the record of the preparation of the Kingdom of God—how God educated a barbarous group of tribes and trained them, stubborn and wicked as they were, for a spiritual purpose of which we see the fulfillment in the New Testament' (*New Commentary*, p. 187). But no, in those days Christianity meant believing in the verbal inspiration of every word of the Old Testament as well as the New—'as if the Bible had come down straight from Heaven, bound in morocco leather, complete with marginal references and archbishop Usher's dates'; and [to] my father who had enquired into the making of the Bible this position was untenable. (2) He had no use for the Church, either from past history or present performance, but considered it always reactionary, ill-advised, the source of the worst wars and discords of history, usually fighting for obscurantism against truth, exploiting the poor for its own ends and making them content with their present miseries by promises of future happiness in another world. He despised those who believed what they were told in any religion, without thinking out things for themselves, and rejecting what reason could not but jib against— ceremonial observances seemed to him mere superstition, and the invocation of saints and the Blessed Virgin as sheer idolatry. He was, however, always tolerant and kind to those who thought otherwise, and allowed my mother later on to become a Christian and never distressed her by showing up what he considered to be weak spots in her creed; but he considered it his duty to do all he could to prevent his children from joining any special Christian Church, and those who did so had to do it against his consent, and without his official knowledge of the fact. In later life he called himself agnostic, and used to go to services at the Unitarian Church in Croydon of which Mr John Page Hopps was minister. But when he was dying, he begged us not to take the name of God in his funeral service, or to put it on his tombstone, as he considered it degrading to cling at the time of death to what he had always considered superstitious. He had come to consider that there must be a First Cause or Creator of the Universe, but he could not flatter himself that this Power occupied Itself with individual men, though he always hoped to know more about It. He was fond of telling us the story of the man who when he was dying called out: 'O God (if there is a God) save my soul (if there is a soul) from hell (if there is a hell)' and considered it a warning to avoid weakness when 'in extremes'!

My father made many friends in England and was deeply impressed by English freedom. He liked the English manner of living, and became a keen politician and an ardent feminist, and resolved never to go back to Hindu ways, but to bring his wife out of purdah, and if he had children, to give them all education on English lines, and in England if he could ever afford it. He passed all his examinations successfully, was called to the Bar on 11 June 1867, and returned to India in November 1868 to begin his career as barrister at the Calcutta High Court.

2.4

Return to Calcutta

In the meantime, as has been said, my poor mother was not having a happy life during my father's absence. She was repeatedly blamed for being 'unlucky', and she used to practice all sorts of austerities and perform all sorts of penances to make up for his having lost his caste by going to England. In fact those hysterical attacks already described were probably due in great measure to all her religious activities. She suffered vicariously during all the years of his absence.

On my father's way home in November 1868, he got the news of his father's death, which was a great grief to him. His mother, however, as soon as she saw him forgave him and even wanted him to come back to the family house, but he refused to do this, knowing that he had lost his caste, and therefore it might cause endless difficulties if he came back as if nothing had happened, and he was determined not to go through the formal ceremony of 'Prayaschit' by which he could have been received back into caste. He stayed temporarily at an hotel, and then took a small house in Entally where my mother joined him. Having been brought up as a good Hindu, and taught that a husband's word was law, she was able to make a complete break with the past, though what a terrible effort it must have been to her it is hard to realise. After my father left for England, his father employed a governess to teach my mother and such of his daughters as were home how to read and write, and this lady being a Christian missionary must have taught them something about Christianity. All this time, as has been said, my mother was an extremely devout practising Hindu, and it is hard to find out now when she began to be attracted by Christianity.

Here is inserted a 'note by N.H. Blair' [Janaki's sister, Nellie, in Janaki's hand]:

> I think Mamma first came in contact with Christian teaching when she went to England. There was a governess at Simla House, a missionary lady. I think our grandfather arranged for her to go and teach Mamma and such daughters who were home after Papa left for England (in 1864).
>
> As far as I remember, Papa wished her to become a Christian. He thought it would be easier for her when she had to live in England. She was a very religious woman. You remember how she practiced all sorts of austerities and performed penances when Papa was in England to atone for his going, and I suppose, being such a devoted wife, it was not hard for her, at his request, to adopt Christianity. But I do not think he reckoned with her religious strength of character. Not being himself inclined to adopt any dogmas, he did not realize what an ardent Christian she would become. But when he saw that it came to mean the best part of her life, he never interfered. But, as you know, though he did not object to our being brought up as Christians, he would not allow us to be baptised or confirmed until we were 21.
>
> I don't think Papa minded her being baptised. I believe she was first confirmed in the Church of England because Colonel and Mrs Wood were then members of the Church of England. Afterwards, when they joined the Brethren, Mamma joined them and was baptised by total immersion, when they were living at Anerley. I am sorry I can't tell you when.

2.5

Beginnings of a Life in English Style
1868–74

In afterlife my mother often used to tell us how very difficult she found it to come out of purdah and live in English fashion. In the first place, she had to give up wearing a sari, and to wear English dress, because in those early days, Indian women who went about dressed in saris were considered 'no better than they ought to be'. Then there was the difficulty of food. For an orthodox Brahmin girl to have to eat food cooked and handled by Mahomedan servants, and to have to eat meat—even beef—was a most terrible ordeal, as she had been brought up to think such behavior a most deadly sin. She used to say that she could never have surmounted these difficulties if it had not been for my father's great kindness and consideration. At first, he himself would bring her meals from the kitchen, so that the Mahomedan or low caste Hindu servants should not touch it, and in the desire to save him trouble, she got over her feelings of distaste. Although she and her husband were now 'outcastes' in the sense that their relations could no longer eat with them or take water from their hands, they were all devoted to her and she loved them all just as much as ever, and used to go visit them frequently. Here again a difficulty arose. She could not be seen by her servants and neighbours leaving her house in a sari; but on the other hand she could not arrive at her mother-in-law's or mother's house in an English dress. She solved this problem by taking a sari with her in the carriage, drawing down the blinds and changing on the way, so as to arrive clad in a sari and barefoot. On the way home she had to change back to dress and stockings and shoes, and she went on doing this until her relations got used to her new ways. The English language too, she found extremely difficult, and never really managed to conquer it completely. She had, as has been said, a very retiring and unambitious nature, and it was only her great love and admiration for her husband, and her feeling that whatever he ordered must be right, that enabled her to adapt to his wishes.

My father too had his own difficulties as well as those incurred by teaching his wife to adopt English customs and manners. He and Mr Monomohun Ghose[40] were at that time the only Indian barristers, and it was a hard struggle at first to make both ends meet. He had to work very hard indeed and persevere with his studies when no cases seemed forthcoming, and at the beginning it sometimes seemed doubtful as to whether he would be able to maintain his new establishment. He used to tell us afterwards that one month he had not earned enough to pay his servants' wages in full. He sent for them, and explained this, and told them that they could leave if they liked, and he would pay them the balance due to them as soon as possible. But if they were willing to stay on, he promised that this should never happen again. They all did stay on, and it never did happen again! He soon began to earn a steady income which gradually increased and increased until he became one of the most wealthy and best known barristers in India. As soon as his income allowed of it, he began helping his mother and relatives, and paying off his father's debts; and to please his mother, he had part of the ancestral home—Simla House in Boloram Dey's street—dedicated to the family idol, Radha Kanta, and endowed the idol with a substantial income.

When her first baby was born, my mother began to be much happier and more confident in herself. This baby, a son, was born on March 5th 1870, and there were great rejoicings in the family. My father at that time was a great admirer of the poet Shelley, the apostle of freedom, and the boy was named Kamal Krishna Shelley. The 'Krishna' was out of respect for Raja Binoy Krishna Deb of Sovabazar who was a great friend of my father. Some time after Shelley's birth, my parents moved from Entally to a house in Dalhousie Square South, and there a daughter was born on July 16th 1871 who was named Nalini Heloise and called 'Nellie' for short. This house not proving satisfactory, the next move was to the delightful house with a garden and tanks, still standing—no. 1 Store Road, Ballygunge. Here another daughter Susila Anila (Susie) was born on October 22 1872, and now that his eldest child was getting on for three years old, my father began to make plans for his education and that of the little girls.

2.6

Hemangini's First Visit to England
1874–5

As has been said, my father resolved that his children should be given a full English education, and therefore decided to send them to England as young as possible so that they could learn the language from infancy and be brought up entirely in English ways. For this purpose he wanted to find an English family who would undertake the charge of the children, and through a solicitor named Savage, whom he had met in England, he heard of such a family. Colonel Wood was a retired Army man who had spent a good deal of time in China, and after retiring had settled down in Anerley with his wife and numerous children; and wishing to supplement his meagre pension, agreed to take in my mother and the three children for a year or so, and to take entire charge of the two elder children when my mother went back.

My father could not possibly afford to take his family to England himself, as he was working far too busily to earn enough money to keep them in England, so my poor mother had to take the voyage alone, with three small children, in the summer of 1874, when Shelley was just 4, Nellie nearly 3 and Susila about 18 months old. She often told me what a nightmare that voyage was! My father knew one man who was travelling on the boat, Dr Godeve Chakravati, and asked him to help my mother. He promised to do so, but my mother said he was a terrible snot, and was ashamed of knowing another Indian who could scarcely speak any English, and took absolutely no notice of her! She was terribly seasick and miserable and thoroughly scared. The only bright spot was that my father had written to the P&O agents at every port of call to look after my mother, and they came aboard at each port and helped her in various ways. She said the last straw was when playing with the children one day she asked the baby 'Where's Papa?' and the baby solemnly replied, 'He's dead'! However, at last the voyage came to an end, and she arrived at the Woods, who were then living at 8 Harcourt Road, Anerley.

But unfortunately, neither she nor the children were at all happy with the Wood family. It was a great pity that a family who had lived in the East had been selected, because they had a strong colour prejudice and disliked all orientals, classing them as 'natives', and it was only the generous sum paid by my father that caused them to take in his family. Both my mother and her children were subjected to numerous indignities, and never treated as equals by the family. My mother and Susie always maintained afterward that Colonel and Mrs Wood meant to be kind, and the trouble was caused by their older children, the eldest daughter Harriet being the same age as my mother. The next daughter Edie was not a pleasant person, and the sons were thoroughly unsatisfactory and later broke their parents' hearts by their evil conduct. The amazing part is that my mother never bore a grudge against them, forgave them all the indignities, and was extremely good to all the family later on, when she was wealthy and in an established position in her own house in England, and they were poor and unhappy.

At the beginning of her stay, they certainly did not succeed in making her feel happy and at ease, but she used to say that Edie was the chief offender. Colonel and Mrs Wood did their best, and under their auspices she was baptised in the Church of England, But shortly after this, they both became Plymouth Brethren,[41] and my mother used to go with them to the meetings at the Drill Hall in upper Norwood, and grew to like them better than the Church services—so that, to our lasting regret, she became a most devout member of the 'Brethren' for the whole of her life ... .

After she had been in England a few months, my mother realised that she was going to have another baby, and her fourth child was born at Anerley on 4 December 1874 and named Kalikrishna Wood. She said Mrs Wood was very kind to her at that time, and her own youngest daughter Laura was born at about the same time, and she and Kali became great friends. The eldest daughter Harriet was married to a Mr Bennett shortly afterwards, and went with her husband to settle in America. The other daughters were Edie, Gracie, Nona and Laura, and the two sons Ted and Bob, and they were taught by a governess called Miss Pilditch.

In the autumn of 1875 my father went to England during the long vacation (pujah holidays) to bring back my mother, Susie, and Kali; and Shelley and Nellie were left in England and began doing lessons with the Governess. They seem to have been thoroughly miserable, as will be seen from the following account written by Nellie about a year before her death in 1936.

[The following insert continues in Janaki's hand, and is entitled 'Note by N.H. Blair'.]

> As regards my own early recollections, they are very vague. I think I told you before, I was a little bit 'wanting' as a small child from the age of about two. I know when Mamma left in 1875 I was too stupid to realise it and I believe I played with some little dolls she had given me and never cried at the time, much to the horror of the Woods. I was frightfully severely punished as they thought I was willfully obstinate and stubborn; but on thinking it over now, I believe I was merely stupid—half an idiot. I bear the marks of being pushed under an iron bed which cut open my head. I think I told you I used to be locked up in dark cupboards. When Mamma left in 1878 I don't think I cried then, I felt too badly. Susie I remember did cry. The Woods liked Shelley and Susie much better than they did me. So you see these sort of things would not make interesting reading.
>
> As you say, we have very little information about our Mother. She always kept herself in the background. She must have endured a martyrdom going to England and putting up with the Woods' behavior. Col. and Mrs Wood were fairly decent, but the children's behavior was deplorable. They despised her for being an Indian, for not knowing the language well etc., and she never retaliated. They were decent to my father because he held the purse-strings. I blame Mrs Wood a great deal. I think she used to, in moments of irritation, say things against Mamma and the rest of us, and the children used to let it out. I know it was always impressed upon us that we being Indians were inferior, that our parents paid too little for us in return for what we got, that our hands could not be clean being dark-skinned, etc. etc. They thought

that their parents being Army and Official people were humiliated by having to take 'natives' into their house. Perhaps they did it ignorantly. It is not for us to judge. If they sinned their sins bring their own punishment. I am sure it is being made up to Mamma now for all she suffered both from them and from us. Living with the Woods had so deteriorated the character of we three elder children, that when she did come to England to make a home for us, we were not worthy of her. She came too late to undo the harm. Do you remember in a book by Mrs Molesworth called *Henny*, the latter a small girl was undergoing the same hardening process, but luckily a friend came and prevented any real harm. So that when her mother came she was not injured. Of course had our characters been what they should be, no amount of the Woods' methods could have injured us really. But we were prone to evil and they expedited our path. I was the worst of the three because being stupid I hardened more quickly.

2.7

Kidderpore House, Calcutta
1876–84

When they got back to Calcutta at the end of 1875, my father decided to build a house at Kidderpore, near Calcutta, where his grandfather used to live, and where he himself was born. He was well able to afford to do so, as he had been having amazing success at the Bar. Mr Sachidanand Sinha writes of him: 'Bonnerjee's first brief was in a criminal case in the mofussil. It was one of historic importance as it was a very sensational trial in which Mr (afterwards Lord) McDonnell—later Lieut. Governor of the North West Provinces and Oudh, but then only a subdivisional officer—had charged a fisherwoman with having brought a false case against him. Bonnerjee, appearing for the accused, secured her acquittal from the Court of a British Officer, which was a very notable triumph for him. But he soon turned his attention from mofussil practice in criminal courts to civil work in the High Court. He was retained as a junior in many cases on the original side of the High Court, and soon made his mark as a clever cross-examiner and a skillful reasoner. His practice began to rise, and he soon acquired a prominent position and gained the confidence of the Bench, the Bar, and a large circle of clients. He had a hard and uphill task before him, but his perseverance overcame all obstacles. He had no influential friends to take him by the hand, and he owed his immense success to his own energies, talents and industries. At the end of ten years his career was justly regarded as one of phenomenal success. He was the first Indian to attain that distinguished and prominent position. As an advocate, Bonnerjee used to go straight to the point, whether in argument or cross-examination, and his addresses were lucid and straight forward, and never prolix, irrelevant or long-winded. That tact in managing judges and witnesses—which is among the first requisites of a great advocate—he possessed in very remarkable degree. And so within a dozen years of his joining the Bar he had attained the highest success in the vocation he had chosen, and had reached the highest rung on the professional ladder.'

He was a most indefatigable worker, and when not actually in Court, used to spend his spare time reading law and studying cases. I have recently been told that he never refused work of any kind; and there is a story told about him that when he once overheard a very junior barrister refusing to take up a brief because it was only marked at two gold mohurs, he afterwards very courteously told the client that he would be glad to undertake it himself. The junior barrister never forgot that lesson and was grateful for it.

Kidderpore House was begun in 1876 and finished the following year, and my father and mother and children enjoyed living more or less in the country, although it was rather malarious, and they suffered fever sometimes. In 1878 my mother had another infant, a boy, but it was born dead. That same year, in the autumn, they went to England again, to leave Susie behind for her education, as she was now six years old. She was a high-spirited child, very clever, and afraid of nobody, and got on much better with the Woods than Nellie. She became very fond of Mrs Wood, and used to call her Auntie, and kept up with the girls of the family all her life, and often used to go and see them after she was grown up. Many of her trials were from the great strictness of the up-bringing, for Colonel and Mrs Wood after becoming Plymouth Brethren decided that theatre-going, parties and even novel-reading were all wrong and 'worldly', so their poor children and the young Bonnerjees had a very dreary life with very few pleasures. Once Nellie went to stay with some friends of the Woods for some reason or other, and in the house found a volume of *Arabian Nights*—her first taste of fiction. She read all through it with the greatest eagerness, and when she got back told all the stories to the other two, to their great pleasure and excitement. That wonderful memory and gift of story-telling Nellie retained to the end of her life.

Shelley was in a constant state of rebellion, and his sisters were always trying to shield him from the wrath of the authorities, and all their pocket money went in helping him out of scrapes. He became so naughty and unmanageable that at last the Woods confessed that they could not cope with him, and as a punishment he had better be sent to school. He told me how very delighted he was to hear of this 'punishment' and how thankful he was to be sent away from the Woods to school. But this was not until 1881 when he was 11 years old, and was sent to a preparatory school for Rugby kept by a man called Veckery.⁴²

My parents went back to India that same year, 1878, after leaving Susie, and on 2 October 1879 their third son was born and named Saral Krishna Keats, called 'Kittie' for short. He grew up into a very high-spirited and enterprising and rather wild boy, and Kali, although five years older, admired him immensely for his exploits and narrow escapes.

My father was working very hard all this time, and conducted another rather sensational case in 1877—that of Gopal Lall Lett against Tarini Chand Bysack which was eventually decided by the Judge, Mr Justice Macpherson, in his favour.⁴³

On 5 January 1881, a third daughter arrived, named Pramila Florence, and in the March of that year my father was appointed to act a standing counsel. This was the first time an Indian had achieved this high post, and my father officiated on four different occasions, March 1881 to November 1882; March 1882 to December 1884; and again in 1886 and in 1887.

My father was a great philanthropist, and an account of his many charities would fill a whole book.⁴⁴ He was continually helping students to educate themselves, giving money for 'shradh' ceremonies,⁴⁵ helping other barristers, paying off people's debts, as well as supporting most of his relatives and paying the expenses of the marriage ceremonies of all their daughters.

Both he and my mother were very fond of all their relations, who used to come often to see them at Kidderpore; and he used to visit his mother once a week, and my mother used to go constantly to both Simla House and Bowbazar. About this time, his eldest sister's daughter Benodini became a child widow, and he decided that she should be married again, so he found a suitable Brahmin husband for her, who was a Brahmin by faith and willing to marry a widow. Of course none of the rest of my aunts' families could eat with her again, so she used to go to my mother at Kidderpore House, and I fancy her eldest son Kalyan was born there around 1881. My mother was very fond of her and her husband and children and did a great deal for them.

In 1882, a third visit was paid to England and this time Kali was left behind. On 28 July 1883, the fourth son, Ratna Krishna Curran was born, and in 1884 another visit was paid to England.

※ 2.8

6 Park Street, Calcutta
1885

About this time, a scheme was on foot in Calcutta for extending the Kidderpore Docks, and for this purpose the Government wished to acquire all the land upon which Kidderpore House stood. My mother told me afterwards that although this was a great disappointment at the time, it was the best thing that could have happened. The place was malarious and they were beginning to feel the distance from the town as a drawback, especially when it was a case of doctors being sent for medicine and brought out. They now had to look about for a new abode, and when my mother was in England in 1884, my father bought a large house at no. 6 Park Street, in what was then the very best part of Calcutta. It was a really beautiful mansion (no other word is grand enough) and had been Sir Elijah Impey's dwelling house, and the imposing gate had sphinxes on each side, put up by him. A long drive, flanked on one side by a row of servant's godowns discretely hidden behind a hedge, and on the other by an enormous coach-house, led up to the house, with its huge portico and imposing marble entrance hall and beautiful wooden staircase (with 80 steps?) built with galleries on each floor. On the ground floor was a large state dining room in the centre, to the east of which was a suite of three rooms: ante room, study, and bedroom, and a bathroom; to the west was a lesser dining room with a still smaller children's dining room beyond it; and to the west of this, a second suite of three rooms similar to the first. These rooms all led to a deep south verandah, with steps going down to the garden. The middle storey consisted of an enormous billiard room, part of which was screened off and used as an extra sitting room, over the portico; a huge central drawing room, with a suite of bedroom, ante room and bathroom on each side of it, leading to another deep south verandah, with an extension westwards, over the ground floor western suite of rooms. The top storey was similarly arranged, with an open verandah over the billiard room. Above all was a flat roof which used to be a favourite playground for the smaller children.

My mother did not see this house before she left, and she used to get ecstatic letters from her relations about the wonderful property; and one of her brothers wrote and told her that one could drive a coach and four along the verandah—which I believe was literally true! There was a pleasant garden with a tennis court on the east of the house, and a range of stables beyond it with stalls for eleven horses; and to the north of the house a flower garden, with narrow paths and two fern houses. On the west and south were narrow paths only. My parents became very fond of this lovely house, and in it my mother died in 1910, so it sheltered the family for many years. I was born there in 1886, and all Shelley's children were born there, and two of Ratan's—Bhatan and Protap—so it was considered a family dwelling. It was to this house that my parents came back in 1884 with Kittie, Pramila (Milly) and Ratan (called Tinymite by my mother and Teenie by the rest of the family, because when Milly first saw him she said: what a tiny mite of a baby!). They had sent Shelley to Rugby School in 1883, and Nellie and Susie and Kali were still with the Wood family.

2.9

The Founding of the Congress
1885

At the beginning of the eighteen-eighties, a movement was springing up amongst the educated men in India generally and especially in Bengal, towards a desire for political advancement. Since the conquest of India by England, the Indian Intelligentsia had been more or less passive under English rule, but education on English lines had been rapidly spreading, and young Indian men had been going to England for education there. All this had been arousing in these young men and others a sense of the duties they owed to themselves and their country. This movement was not only, as Lala Rajpat Rai once remarked, indigenous from within, but was fostered by a number of distinguished English men, including the former Viceroy, Lord Dufferin. Other outstanding names are those of Mr A.O. Hume, Mr George Yule, Sir William Wedderburn, and Sir Henry Cotton.[46]

My father's first appearance in political life was in 1883 when he presided at a great demonstration at the Calcutta Town Hall. This was 'to approve of Lord Ripon's policy in having been able to save at least the principle of the then famous but now almost forgotten "Ilbert Bill" in the face of the most influential British agitation that had ever been organized in India'.[47] He proved himself an eloquent speaker, and when in December 1885 the first sitting of the Indian National Congress was held in Bombay, he was elected as the first President. The aims of the Congress as stated by him in the Inaugural Address were:

(a) The promotion of personal intimacy and friendship amongst all the more earnest workers in our cause in the different parts of the empire.

(b) The eradication by direct friendly personal intercourse of all possible race, creed, or provincial prejudices amongst all lovers of our country, and the fuller development and consolidation of these sentiments of national unity that had their origin in their beloved Lord Ripon's ever memorable reign.

(c) The authoritative record, after this has been carefully elicited by the fullest discussion, of the matured opinion of the educated classes in India on some of the more important and pressing of the social questions of the day.

(d) The determination of the lines upon, and methods by which, during the next twelve months, it is desirable for native politicians, to labour in the public interest. This Congress was to meet once a year in different cities.[48]

This 'Indian National Congress' had its Jubilee in December 1935, and reading the accounts of the Jubilee in the press makes one realise what a lot of water has flowed under the bridge since 1885! As Mr Sachidanand Sinha says: 'Mr Bonnerjee's Presidential Address—so simple and straightforward—shows the great advance the country has made during the last half-century, if contrasted with the public utterances of present-day nationalist leaders which may be summed up in the words "from demand for reform to that of substance of independence".' Independence—swaraj—is now universally recognised as being a sine qua non by all politicians, and indeed by the mass of thinking people; the only debatable points being as to how this will best be obtained; and whether Indians should demand freedom within the empire—dominion status, or complete severance from the empire!

But at the beginning, Indian politicians had to proceed very cautiously, and it is interesting to note how for the first twenty years or so each Presidential address begins with expressions of almost fulsome loyalty, affection, and thankfulness to the British Government!

My father threw himself heart and soul into work for the Congress. He was elected President again in 1892, at Allahabad, and both in India and during his yearly visits to England he used to organize meetings and demonstrations on Indian questions. It was he who interested the late Mr George Yule in the Congress, and Mr Yule was elected President in 1888. Mr Charles Bradlaugh was also brought into the movement by my father, and he attended the Bombay session of 1889, and sponsored an Indian Reform Bill in Parliament.[49] My father worked unceasingly with Mr A.O. Hume, the General Secretary for the same year, over Congress propaganda, and gave large sums of money towards it. After Lord Cross' Reform Bill of 1892, he offered himself as a candidate for a seat in the legislature placed at the disposal of the Senate of the Calcutta University, and won the election against a candidate strongly backed by officialdom.

Mr S. Sinha says again: 'Bonnerjee spoke most perfect English, not only in idiom and form, but also in pronunciation. Though he excelled in forensic eloquence, he was also a powerful platform speaker. I recall even now, forty-seven years after having heard it, his magnificent ... peroration—with which he closed his speech in moving a resolution at the fourth session of the Congress held at Allahabad in 1885 in a voice at once deep, sonorous and well-modulated: "The reforms however for which we have pressed in this resolution," said he, "are not by any means the only reforms which are essential for the welfare of India. They are, perhaps, the simplest and in regard to them the country is now most completely of one mind as to the exact steps that it is necessary for the Government to take. But there are other great and vital reforms which must, sooner or later, have to be dealt with if India is to be justly administered. But at the present moment what we first want is that those simple and clear reforms, which are now fully ready for practical embodiment, should be carried out. Now, listen delegates, do not be cast down, do not be disheartened if immediately you put forward a request and is not granted by those who are responsible for the Government of the country. Be patient, be persistent, be true to your cause and to yourselves. Remember that even now there are many reforms about which large majorities are agreed in England, but which the English people have not yet got. If you are true to yourselves, if you are persistent, and if you go on agitating and agitating you will be sure to get what you are asking for. Bide your time, and then give a long pull, a strong pull, and a pull altogether, and you will unfailingly land yourselves triumphant on the shores of victory." Reading this splendid peroration in cold print, even today after a lapse of nearly half a century, one endowed with some imagination can well visualize the enthusiasm and the storm of applause it evoked in the Congress, and brought down the House such as I have seldom seen.'

2.10

Family Life at 6 Park Street

As this is only a Family Chronicle, and not a political history of the times, enough has been said to indicate my father's interests and activities at this time. He was brought by his political works into contact with many new and interesting personalities. My mother too while remaining essentially domestic in all her tastes was obliged to come forward and act as hostess on several occasions. She was always very shy and nervous at such times, but enjoyed small parties and entertaining my father's intimate friends. She enjoyed a good gossip with her own relations, and was shrewd in her judgments of people's characters, and—when at her ease, had a keen sense of humor. The 6 Park Street house was beautifully furnished in solid mid-Victorian style, and all the appointments were in keeping and of the choicest character. My father had his crockery and cutlery and linen specially made for him in England, and we still have some pieces of his once famous Coalport china dinner service with a large monogram of W.C. and H.B. in the centre of each plate and dish; and the remains of a beautiful hand-painted dessert service. My father liked to keep 'open house' hospitality, and every Saturday he had a dinner party of friends and rising junior barristers, which was to include the future Lord Sinha ... and others to mix with seniors like Mr K.M. Chatterjee and Mr R. Mitter. Other friends were Mr Umakali Mukerjee, Sir Tarak Nath Palit, Mr N.C. Bose.... He was particularly fond of his eldest sister's husband Babu Sasi Bhusan Mukerjee who was Government Pleader of Bhagalpur, and of his wife's brother-in-law Girish Chunder Mukerjee, always called Dhurmas Babu, who was Superintendent to the Accountant General of Bengal. Another friend was Mr Monomohun Ghose, and my father used to stay with the Ghose family at Krishnagur—Mr B.L. Gupta and Mr R.C. Dutt and Mr O.C. Mullick and Sir K.G. Gupta were all lifelong friends of his.[50]

On 26 June 1886 I was born at 6 Park Street and named 'Janaki Agnes Penelope'. My father had been in Delhi on a case shortly before my birth and was amused to find how common a name Janaki was in the north, though in Bengal it was never given to girls because Janaki and Sita, the heroine of the Ramayana, was such an unlucky person. There was a Janaki living near where he was staying, and he used to hear people calling continually 'Janaki Bibi, Janaki Bibi hay', so he told my mother if the new baby was a girl she must be called Janaki. The 'Agnes Penelope' was after Mrs Wood, so, for my sins, I was saddled with one Indian, one English and one Greek name. I was always called Baby, until I was nearly eighteen, or 'Bee' as short for Baby. In addition to this, my father called me 'Benjamin', as the youngest of a large family, and 'Babiole' from a person in a book he had enjoyed. Before I could speak plainly I used to substitute 'N' for 'L' and so called myself 'Babione' and from this came 'Oni' which was my father's pet name for me always. It used to be a family joke when I was very small to ask me my name and hear me say 'Janaki Agnes Penelope Babiole Benjamin Onie Bonnerjee.' My father was very fond of giving people nicknames by which he called them ... . Nellie was always Nannie or Nenima, Susie was Jam, Kali Kay or Kakes, Millie was Milesweri, Teenie, Tanaji Malasrai ... —all from small incidents long forgotten. People were proud of their nicknames, and those friends or relatives who were not given special names by him used to feel very hurt about it!

My mother brought back English nurses for the children when she went to England. The first one was called Rose, but she got ill, and then a nurse called Fanny was engaged who stayed with us for many years and only left to get married. Later on, she married a Coal Heaver on the L.S.W. Railway called Reed, and we used to stay with her sometimes at Weymouth, and she and Reed and the children used to come and stay with us in Croydon. Her sister married a hair dresser called Pike, also living at Weymouth, and I remember the thrill of going to play in the hair dressing saloon for hours, and fiddling with all the gadgets there that seemed so wonderful then but would be laughed at now. But this is anticipating.

Shortly before my birth my youngest brother Teenie aged nearly three had been very ill from some sort of digestive trouble. (I remember being told by somebody that he swallowed a cork which had swelled inside him! But I fancy the illness was due to a less sensational cause really). He much resented the arrival of the new baby, and when asked one day what he would like to eat demanded the new baby's head as a meal! Fanny was in charge of him and Milly. The latter was devoted to Fanny, who adored her. Milly was the prettiest and most attractive member of the family, and the most high-spirited, and rapidly became the most popular. I well remember the amusement in the family, when we were all settled in Croydon, when Mrs Stevens, the wife of the man who made all the family boots and shoes, and who had a peculiar nasal accent, told my mother that without any doubt Milly was the 'flair' of the family! She was just five and a half when I was born, and at that time my father used to call her Mother Bunch. My Mother often told us how proud she was of her well-balanced family—four boys and four girls, and an elder brother to look after each sister. I think these years about which I am now writing must have been the Golden Age of my parents—my father was at the very top of the tree in his profession, with all his political interests and new friends. The eldest son was doing well at Rugby, the girls were very clever and rapidly acquiring English culture, the youngest children were at hand to play with, and the nursery was presided over by a nice English nurse; the relations were all admiring, and grateful for monetary help, and all the prospects for the future were bright.

2.11

Settling in England
1888

But now some changes were contemplated. The Woods had moved to Croydon and had taken a house at 44 Lansdowne Road. There was an excellent High School for Girls in Croydon and my elder sister began going there as a day-scholar in 1884, and as the family was now so numerous my father decided that the best thing would be for my mother to settle completely in England for our education, and he would come over every autumn during the Pujah holidays. The Woods wanted to give up the house, so my parents decided to take it over from them 'lock stock and barrel,' while looking about for a suitable property to purchase for themselves. My mother must have hated the idea of such a complete break with her present life and such separation from my father, but she never complained, and they must both have felt that it would not do to get any more out of touch with their elder children, who were—naturally enough—more or less strangers to their parents.

Accordingly, in the spring of 1888 my mother sailed on the Kaiser-i-Hind with Kitty, Milly, Teenie, and myself and Fanny, and took over no. 44 Lansdowne Road. That autumn Shelley went up to Oxford, to New College[51]; the two elder girls who had been attending the High School for a year or so took Milly there with them. Kali and Kitty were sent to a tutor called Mr Lute in Addiscombe Road, and Teenie to a kindergarten kept by a Madame Macalis and her daughter Mimi, which was afterwards taken over by Miss Cartwright.

When my father came over for his holidays, the search for a house began, and a suitable property was found not far from Lansdowne Road, and even nearer the High School. The property was bought, and numerous additions and alterations were made to it, and the result was an exceedingly comfortable and roomy family dwelling house, in which we lived for twenty years, only selling it after my father's death.

The house, no. 8 Bedford Park, Croydon, was named 'Kidderpore' by us, after the first Kidderpore house, and stood in the middle of about an acre of garden. It was a four-minute walk from East Croydon station, and less from the High School, and the Whitgift Grammar School where Teenie went later on. The neighbourhood was then a very good one, though it has deteriorated sadly now, and there were similar large houses all along Bedford Park with nice families living in them. Now, these houses are no longer dwelling houses. No. 4 is a Labour Exchange, one is a club, and one a nursing home, and 'Kidderpore' itself is an orphanage for daughters of Army men! But in those days, as has been said, it was a very pleasant and convenient neighbourhood, only a twenty-minute train journey from London, and yet with lovely country walks within easy reach, and excellent shops. The garden had three high solid wooden gates set in a high brick wall, which ensured great privacy and prevented any overlooking from the road. One was the 'Visitors' Entrance' and opened on to a circular drive, with a lawn on the right (north) and the house straight in front. The second and narrower gate opened on to a flagged path leading to the steps down to the basement entrance of the house, and was marked 'Tradesmen's Entrance,' and the third gate opened on to a stable yard adjoining the two-storied stable building, with stalls for two horses and a harness room below, and quarters for a groom and coachman, and a large hayloft above. As we never kept horses, the yard was used for dogs, and a long row of kennels was built there; one of the upper rooms was used as a dark room for photography, and the hayloft was our favourite place for games. The garden was more or less triangular in shape and the stables were at the apex of the triangle, and the hayloft window overlooked no less than five roads, as our house was the last one in Bedford Park—Bedford Park, Sydenham Road North (leading to South Norwood), Bedford Place (leading to Lansdowne Road), Dingwall Road (leading to the Station) and Sydenham Road, (leading to the High School), the south wall of our garden going down this road. So from this window we could watch all the passersby, and a great game was to stand there with a peashooter and shoot peas upon unsuspecting folk and duck down before one could be seen. I remember, much later on, one of Teenie's school friends Jack Bright (a grandson of the famous John Bright) becoming a perfect adept at this, and when at least one man turned back to make a complaint at the house, he realised what was going to happen and rushed back to help my mother receive this tiresome individual, and wonder with her who could have been the culprit!

But, to continue my description of the house,—between the stables and the main building was a large vegetable garden where we grew potatoes, cabbages, cauliflowers, rhubarb, asparagus and other vegetables as well as strawberries and raspberries; and all around there were numerous apple, pear, cherry and plum trees as well as gooseberry bushes, and white and red and black currant bushes. On the walls were nectarines and peaches, and on the south (Sydenham Road) side of the vegetable garden were two glass hot houses for delicate plants, which communicated with the stable yard through a potting shed. On the south side of the house was a full-sized tennis lawn, shut off from the vegetable garden by a flower bed and a row of lilac and laburnum trees. On the other lawn, to the north of the house, we used to play croquet or practise cricket, and at the Bedford Park end of this lawn was a house where my mother kept poultry, and two rabbit hutches for our rabbits and guinea pigs. The circular drive from the front gate of the house was flanked by two long banks; one, between the drive and the south lawn, was planted with lovely rose trees, and the other between the drive and the servants' entrance was planted with snapdragon every summer, and had a tall poplar tree in the middle of it. All along the walls were lime trees, and flower borders, both on the road walls, and the long wall beyond the lawn, separating our garden from the next door garden was a row of poplar trees. The house must have a chapter to itself.

2.12

Kidderpore, Croydon

As bought by my father, no. 8 Bedford Park was a three-storied house with drawingroom, diningroom and study, ten bedrooms, and a capacious basement with a separate entrance, consisting of a large servants' hall, kitchen, scullery, larder, store cupboard, wine and coal cellar, pantry and china closet. But there was no bathroom at all, and only one lavatory, except for a small servants' one in the basement! [52] This was shocking to Indian ideas, so a bathroom was added on the first floor landing, and two more lavatories; and an extra wing was built for the house containing a billiard and smoking room. A passage leading to these rooms was made at the end of the drawing room, and a small additional sitting room overlooking the drive and front gate, which was used by the three younger children for playing in and doing their lessons, etc., and where our mother used to sit with us when our father was away. When he was in Croydon she always sat with him in the smoking room, which the elder children used as a sitting room also, and the study was made over to the elder sisters as their study work room. The servants' hall was called the schoolroom, and at one time we younger children used to play there, and a rocking horse was kept there. But it was very rarely used by us, and later on my elder sisters fitted it up as a chemical laboratory and used to do experiments there sometimes.

The whole house was beautifully furnished by a London firm called Fox and Co., with good solid furniture, thick nailed-down carpets in every room and on the stairs, as was the fashion in those days. It made an exceedingly comfortable family home, though it was not of course half so grand or luxurious as the Calcutta house.

My mother was a most competent housekeeper, as has been said, and everything in her province went on oiled wheels. There was never any servant trouble, as the same servants stayed on for years. Of course they used to quarrel among themselves sometimes, and there were various difficulties to cope with, but they always adored my mother. The food too was always of the choicest quality, and she invariably gave us the earliest strawberries, green peas, oysters etc., that were in the market. From her Hindu upbringing she used to enjoy giving us special food for special days, and we always had pancakes on Shrove Tuesday, and roast goose at Michaelmas. And Christmas Day used to be a time of gorging for the whole family, my mother making a special expedition to London to get as many dainties as possible from the Army and Navy Stores.

But at best it must have been a lonely and unhappy life for her. As has been said, she was very much out of touch with her eldest children, who rather despised her lack of education—education having been made a fetish by them—and really had nothing in common with her, as they scarcely remembered their life in India and the relatives there. All their pleasures and interests were away from her, and though they tried to do their duty by her, there was at first a lack of spontaneity about it. The youngest children were only too ready to take their tone from the elders, and book learning and culture were the order of the day. The elders were all very clever, and used to bring their equally brilliant friends home in the holidays, and my mother used to like some of them very much. But apart from all this, it was not usual in those days for parents to be friends with their children. They were authorities, and a race apart, and my mother must sadly have missed my father and her own contemporaries.[53]

Her consolations were in writing long diary letters to my father every day with minute accounts of all the daily doings, and in receiving equally long letters from him every week about his doings, and in her religion [sic]. As has been said, under the auspices of Colonel Wood and Mrs Wood she joined the Plymouth Brethren and became a firm and a devoted adherent to this sect. She used to go, and take all her children to their meeting house in Croydon, which was called the Iron Room and situated in a very slummy part of the town, about half-an-hour's walk from Bedford Park. The Brethren were mostly lower middle class,— respectable tradesmen and the like, with very little education. Our own gardener, Walter Grouch, with his wife and daughter were members. There were a few people of our own standing, but very few. How dreary those Sunday meetings were it is painful to remember. The elders used to relieve their boredom by trying to 'catch out' the speakers and noting down their mistakes, but we younger ones used to conceal secular books under our Bibles and read them there, or else try to do our Scripture homework then.

I should mention that my father's eldest sister's eldest son, Satish Mookerjee, was sent to Cambridge about this time, and afterwards studied law in London and became a barrister, and used to make our house his home during the holidays, and was just like one of our brothers. He was a few years older than Shelley. Kali was sent to Rugby in the autumn of 1889, and Nellie went to Girton that same year.

Sundays were special days at Kidderpore. They were started with breakfast in bed, as when the elder sisters began their medical work in London they had a very early start and a late return all the week and liked to get up late on Sundays to make up, and we younger ones thought it a marvellous idea, so my mother would send up as many as six trays sometimes! Attendance at the Iron Room was compulsory for the younger ones, and on our return we usually found two or three young Indian students and other friends awaiting us who had arrived for lunch—Mr K.N. and Mr P. Chaudhuri were frequent visitors, also Basanta Mullick and his brothers, Sir B.C. Mitter, Sir B.L. Mitter, Mr C.C. Ghose, and a great many others. After lunch some of us always had to go with my mother to the cemetery, and then there was a 'spread tea' in the dining room and after that 'Hymn' in the drawingroom. Each of us in turn chose our favorite hymn, and Nellie played the piano while the rest of the family sang. Sometimes we used the 'Ancient and Modern' Hymn book and sometimes 'Sankey and Moodie's.'[54] Immediately after this ceremony my mother used to go down to the kitchen to cook a real Indian dinner, and as soon as I was old enough I always used to help her. The servants were all given the evening off, and we used to dish up and carry up the things ourselves—my Aunts always sent the spices to us ready ground in tins and we and our visitors all greatly enjoyed this meal. Sometimes my father would come and help, and I remember him and Mr R.C. Dutt[55] once spending the whole evening cooking a wonderful duck curry which no one could eat because it was too highly spiced ('jhal')! At first the servants were rather 'superior' about Indian food, and my mother always left plenty of cold meat and pudding out for their supper. But she gradually noticed that however many curries might be left over on Sunday nights, there was never anything on Monday morning, and at last a deputation came to her from the servants asking her to cook just a little more of everything if she didn't mind, as they all enjoyed it so much!

2.13

Notes by Mrs Arthur Alexander
'The Bonnerjee Family'

I have been asked to tell something of my friendship with S.A.B. (Susie) and also my recollections of the family life in Croydon.

When I was eleven we were living in Finchley, and I attended a day school known as Saxonhurst. During the summer of 1884, as I returned home from morning school I would often see approaching on the other side of the road two young Indians, who I knew were staying at a college tutor's in Finchley. As it was a case of 'idle hands' with them, they were ripe for all kinds of mischief and I had all I could do to keep my countenance and pass them 'head in air' as became a Victorian young lady. Thankfully I record that I never fell below my own standard.[56]

The School held a Sale of Work, with entertainments to raise money for the College Hospital in commemoration of the Jubilee. I had the part of March in the recitation of the months of the year, and I remember that the first three reciters were held up by rounds of applause, led by the two young Indians, as they came on. Then the long holidays came, I saw them no more, and forgot their existence.

... My mother, having lost her husband in December 1884 and her eldest son in March 1888, moved to Croydon, and on the first Sunday as I went up the aisle in the Iron Room, great was my amazement to see the same youth seated at the back row near our seats!

Here it might be well to explain something about the 'Iron Room', the place where we and Mrs Bonnerjee worshipped.

It belonged to a community known as Open Brethren. This was a name given to them by outsiders because in their desire to get away from the many schisms of Christianity, a number of earnest people about the year 1830 in different parts of England and Ireland, all unknown to each other, had begun to meet together simply as Christians coming from all sorts of denominations and calling each other Brothers and Sisters in Christ. They had no set ministers, but held that every true believer is indwelt by the Holy Spirit of God, and if *subject* to the Holy Spirit may be led to minister helpfully to others, though this ministry was strictly confined to men (1 Cor. 12:14). Gradually, the movement spread, and now all over the world where Christianity has been received, such gatherings may be met with. It has been a movement to return to Apostolic conditions as described in the book of the Acts. It is an Ideal, and if it fails it is because of the failure of the human factor, not of the Heavenly Lord. The local gathering of these Christians is generally spoken of as an Assembly. They are keen on mission work at home and abroad, and though there are no paid officials, in every assembly there will be found one Brother who takes responsibility for getting preachers and teachers for the Community and another who is superintendent of Sunday School, and another who looks after the finance represented by free-will offerings, usually generously and conscientiously contributed. The poor are also looked after. The Sunday morning Service always takes the form of the Lord's Supper, and those who minister do so as led by the Holy Spirit; and when all are conscious of the Lordship of Christ, the Meeting rises to a very high level of spiritual worship. Unhappily sometimes there are those who are not spiritually minded, and are self-assertive, and then there is disappointment. The years 1890 to 1900 were not very happy years for the Iron Room Assembly owing to the presence of certain ill-regulated and opinionated men, and so no strong appeal was made to Mrs Bonnerjee's family, and no one but herself ever came into what is known as the 'Fellowship'. I have always felt it was a great disgrace to us as a Community, and feel we failed the Lord in this respect.

 I still continue in the same Fellowship, though in other places where my lot has been cast, and have always found far more ideal conditions than in Croydon. My father-in-law, H.W. Alexander, was a responsible Brother at the Iron Room, and I honestly believe he died from a heart attack brought on through distress about meeting matters. We had left the neighborhood before that.

In May 1888 I started at the Croydon High School, and found that among other new entrants was a little Indian girl called 'Nellie Bonnerjee', who was escorted by an elder sister who was called Susie. I don't know when we first spoke to each other, but soon after I was asked to help with the Infant Class at the Iron Room Sunday School, and I found that Susie was also helping. There were forty children on the register, and she and I, and two other girls had ten each. So we met and spoke Sunday by Sunday and acknowledged each other at school.

Then Mrs Bonnerjee became friendly with my mother and asked me to mid-day dinner each day during Cambridge Local [Examinations] in 1888. I was sitting for Junior and Susie was also. The family was then living in Lansdowne Road, Mrs Bonnerjee having taken over the Woods' house as a running concern. I remember being quite entranced with my experience, as the conversation was most amusing and racy. I was introduced to Shelley Bonnerjee and Satish Mookerjee, both down from Oxford, and Kali Bonnerjee home from Rugby, but gave no sign of ever having seen them before, and they remained equally silent. Here I would like to say that one reason I always so enjoyed being a guest at Mrs Bonnerjee's was because I got a glimpse of a world to me then unknown. I was not a stranger to well-appointed houses and wealthy, but I had never met any young University men; and though there was plenty of fun and joking, there was always a good deal of intelligent conversation, and the thrust and parry was often very diverting. Susie was particularly well able to hold her own, sometimes fighting with the foils off, when she made her opponents squirm.

During the following Easter holidays I spent a lot of time with the family. We had a good many tramps after primroses and to exercise the four dogs then in great favour—a Prince Charles spaniel of Nellie's [called Jumbo or Jummie for short]; a Collie by the name Mopsy belonging to Susie; Bob, a wire-haired terrier; and Simon, a dandy-dinmont of Shelley's.

On one occasion we had a day's drive to Dorking and Box Hill, and we had dinner at the 'White Horse', Dorking, and in the middle there was a gory fight between Bob and Simon, and the girls of the party had to retire to a bedroom with the salad oil bottle to bathe and bind up the wounded—but one at a time be it said! It was that day that Shelley asked me if I had ever lived in Finchley, and I became certain it had not been a case of mistaken identity.

After that the friendship between Susie and me ripened fast. I do not know what she saw in me to attract her, but am certain she had a very warm affection which never appeared to diminish. I delighted in her society and marvelled at her sympathetic understanding. She thoroughly appreciated my religious conviction, and would talk freely upon sacred matters. Though well-to-do, she always understood and considered the fact that I had little spare cash, and if she made plans for us both which were beyond my resources, managed to help so delicately that one's self-respect was never hurt.

Susie was naturally quick-tempered and at times rather irritable (chiefly through physical weakness I believe), but I never had a sharp retort from her, nor was there ever the slightest breeze in our friendship. We never made up a difference because we never had one. I do not mean we never differed—that would be impossible for two people of strong personality, but we had sufficient respect for each other's conviction to give the benefit of the doubt. I remember telling Susie when Arthur Alexander had begun to pay me marked attention, and she was so pleased, and said she was sure we should be happy because we had a similar outlook in things religious as well as equality in social standing. Years later, when during the War our son chose to be a Wireless Officer in the Mercantile Marine to save life rather than a soldier to take it, she said: 'I am very glad Grace, it is the logical outcome of the Christian outlook of his parents and grandparents.'

So in every crisis of my life, her sympathy was sure and sincere.

Susie looked to do good quietly, and often professed a callousness and indifference she was far from feeling. She never 'wore her heart on her sleeve' and we both agreed we did not care for demonstration and so—great as was our friendship—we rarely kissed one another. But after a visit to India she would seek me out immediately, or invite me to call if in the neighbourhood. We corresponded regularly and my last letter was written within three months of her death, which came as a crushing blow to me, yet I think I rejoiced that she was spared failing powers and gradual decay.

To my mind she was a remarkable character, for when quite young she lived at home, helped her mother in choosing dresses, supervised the wardrobes of her younger sisters, took her younger brothers to safe amusements, and incidentally attended lectures, walked to the hospital, and took her medical degree. She was the clever daughter of a clever father who showed his marvellous intellectual powers as much by his attention to and knowledge of detail concerning every member of his family living in England while he was in India, as in the conduct of his profession wherein he took premier rank.

I often thought that wealth was a great drawback to his elder children, because since they already possessed a sufficiency, the stimulus for achievement and the necessary self-control were lacking.

This record would be incomplete without an appreciation of another personality—Mrs Bonnerjee. Though possessed of wealth she was one of the simplest of people in her tastes, of great kindness of heart and liberality. One beautiful memory I have of her was how she daily gathered her household and visitors for the morning reading of the Bible and prayer, and everyone present must have reverenced her. Then, on Sunday afternoons and evenings all the servants were set free, and in the evening Mrs Bonnerjee prepared an Indian meal for family and guests. What an oasis Kidderpore must have been to the dozens of young Indian students in London who came there on Sundays and were transported in spirit to their own country! Daily Mrs Bonnerjee wrote a diary of events to her husband when away. She managed her large household, her banking account, and her children better and more conscientiously than many Englishwomen. She exercised her children's numerous dogs when they were away from home and knitted steadily in odd minutes.

2.14

Life in Croydon
The Final Sorrow
1890

Mrs Alexander's notes give a very good idea of our life in Croydon, with the older children coming home for the holidays from University and School, and the younger ones going to Day Schools in the town. My sister Susie was then still living at home and struggling to get through the London Matriculation, as the years spent with a Governess before she went to the High School were not conducive to make examination work easy. She was exceedingly kind to the younger members of the family, but kept us in very good order and we were afraid of her sharp tongue and critical eye. But praise from her was very welcome and we excited ourselves to win her approval. She chose all our clothes and our books, and helped us with our lessons, and took us to the theatres and entertainments. She always said that her own childhood had been so dull and drab that she was determined that we should have a good time. It was she who taught me to read at the age of four, and began giving me music lessons when I was just six years old. Things were always much more exciting when she was there. Our mother was always a kind comfortable figure in the background, but it was to Susie we went when we wanted things done.

Though my mother's life seemed so prosperous and happy on the surface, except for the inevitable separation from her husband, she really had many worries and anxieties to cope with, and not the least of these were due to my brother Shelley. As has been said, he never got on with the Woods, and as they found him unmanageable, he was sent to school when he was eleven, first to the Preparatory School and then to Rugby. He was not very good at games and played as little as he could, but was brilliant at his books, and went up the school much too rapidly. There was a rule at Rugby then that no boy could be moved into the sixth form until he was sixteen, but Shelley found himself in the form below the sixth, called the Twenty, waiting for promotion to the sixth form long before that, and he had to spend several terms with practically nothing to do except go over old work. Naturally both work and character began to deteriorate with so little to do, and he got into a bad set, and drinking and gambling used to be carried on secretly. The authorities discovered this, and several boys, including Shelley, were threatened with expulsion. My mother, when she heard this, went straight to the Headmaster and managed to induce him not to expel her son and thus wreck all hopes of a University career, and was successful in her appeal. But one can imagine the effort it must have been to a shrinking retiring nature like hers. At Oxford too, he had heavy debts, and there were several explosions of which my mother had to bear the brunt. But yet, he always was her favourite child. He knew exactly how to treat her, with a kind of bantering affection, and always 'got round' her. Nellie and Susie used to complain, the latter with some bitterness, that all their dutiful care and obedience failed to obtain the same response as Shelley's careless teasing.

But all these worries and anxieties were nothing as compared with the great sorrow that was to overwhelm her in December 1890 when my brother Kitty died of double pneumonia after a short illness. He was an eighth-month's baby, and must have had a weak constitution [sic]. When he was sent to bed with a feverish cold early in December, my mother never realised that it was going to be anything serious, and had the greatest difficulty in keeping him in bed. He was a very high-spirited, rather wild boy, as has been said—full of fun and mischief and all sorts of pranks, but very loveable. I can just remember him as being very kind to me, and a great refuge from Teenie's teasing, and my first memory at all is of the extreme pleasure of scribbling on a slate in chalk instead of a dull slate-pencil, under his auspices, when, I think, we were recuperating from whooping cough together.

He was just eleven when he died, and my mother was completely frustrated with grief. She never really got over the shock, and wore mourning for the rest of her life. Susie, then just eighteen, was the only responsible one at home, as well as Satish, and she had to make all the arrangements, cable my father, send for Shelley from Oxford and Nellie from Cambridge, and send a telegram to Kali's House Master at Rugby saying, 'Break to Bonnerjee that his brother is dead and send him home at once,' besides trying to comfort and support my mother. He was buried in the Croydon Cemetery, one of the Brethren from the Iron Room officiating at the funeral. Before he was taken away, we all went into the room to see him lying there, and sang his favorite hymn 'Hark hark my soul,' and my mother was brought in by Shelley in the most pitiable state of grief. That is a scene I can never forget, though I was only four years old.

My mother's sorrows were by no means done with, for at about this time my father was taken seriously ill with rheumatic fever, and the cousins who were staying at 6 Park Street on purpose to look after him and provide for his comfort, were most neglectful. Luckily one of his sisters found this out, and nursed him devotedly so that he made a good recovery. But my mother was of course beside herself with anxiety all the time. When he came to England for the first time after Kitty's death, she would not go out to meet him as usual, saying that she had failed in her trust, because he had left his son under her care and she had let him die. But after that sad meeting was once over she felt a little comforted for the first time. Yet the grief remained with her all her life almost as poignantly as at first and she never really recovered from it. Every Sunday, and on the birth and death anniversaries all her life she used to take flowers to his grave, and when she talked of his death she would cry heartily even to the end of her life.

Shortly after the funeral, the whole family went to Bournemouth for Christmas and the New Year, to make a little change for my mother, and as a conventional 'Merrie Christmas' at home was unthinkable. After that, the threads had to be picked up again, and life went on more or less as usual. My mother's only comfort at this time was in her religion. She used to have 'Mothers' Meetings' on Thursday afternoons, to which several ladies would come for a religious talk, Bible reading and discussion, etc, followed by tea; and she carried these meetings on for many years, and used to enjoy them. I remember Mrs Harling (Grace

Alexander's mother), Mrs Alexander, Mrs Brown (mother of Dr Edith Brown, still Principal of the Medical College at Ludhiana)[57] and some other ladies from the Iron Room used to come regularly, and a Mrs Frith who was a member of St. Matthews' Church nearby. She was a charming old lady with a very gushing manner, which we used to laugh at and copy secretly, and she and my mother were devoted to each other.

In the summer of 1891 my father came over early, and we all went to spend the summer holidays at a place called Dolgelly (pronounced Dolgethby) in North Wales, not far from Barmouth, and had a very happy time there.

2.15

College Friends
Nellie's and Shelley's Engagements
1892

At Oxford, Shelley got to know a man called George Blair, who was somewhat older than himself. George began taking an interest in Shelley partly because the College Tutor asked him to see if he could exert any influence over him to prevent his rather extravagant goings on. When he heard about the family and the wonderful mother who gave up everything for the sake of her children—himself being devoted to his own mother, he became even more interested in the family. ... [he] was very glad to accept an invitation to stay with them. His was a most sterling character, reliable and sound in every way, not very clever but good at all games and especially at rowing. His lack of interest and success in academic pursuits was a great disappointment to his father, who was a successful businessman in a Bradford firm of Wool Merchants, but who was of a very scholarly nature and was anxious for his son to have all the advantages he had missed through having to take up a business career when very young. So George, the eldest son, was sent first to Bradford Grammar School where he got most disappointing reports for work but brilliant ones for games and sports generally; and then to Cambridge and when he was not very successful there, to Oxford! The second son, Will, who might have been a scholar as he had very good brains, refused to go to college and was put into the business young. There were two other brothers, Andrew and Alec, and one daughter Rotha. George's great wish was to be a soldier, but his mother who had at that time lately lost a daughter of about eleven, a little younger than

George, implored him not to think of it, as then he would have to leave her. So, for her sake he gave up his life's ambition. Luckily, in later life he was able to take up soldiering with a volunteer regiment, the Liverpool Scottish, and thoroughly enjoyed every moment of his work there. When he first came to Croydon he was about 27, very tall and good-looking with a large ginger moustache, and we all liked and admired him very much. He was very good to me, and from that time onwards I always liked him much better than any of my brothers. In the summer of 1892, we spent the summer holidays at Shanklin in the Isle of Wight, and George came too. He had been very much attracted by Nellie from the beginning of his acquaintance with us. She was very good-looking then, with beautiful eyes and a lovely voice and much admired by all the young men who came to Kidderpore, and she enjoyed flirting with them at tennis. When at Shanklin there was some kind of boating accident in which George rescued Nellie, this led very speedily to an engagement between them. But, she stipulated, they could not get married for years and years, as she was going to be a doctor, and he had not yet got a profession.

My father countenanced the engagement, and by his advice George began studying for the Bar with a coach in London. Satish Mookerjee was also studying for the Bar, and when Shelley came down from Oxford in 1892, he also joined the Middle Temple.

Nellie's great friend at Girton was a girl called Gertrude Johnson. She was very clever and very attractive with golden hair and blue eyes, and was a very competent and go-ahead person. Nellie, at that time, had already begun to work for Causes and was (not withstanding the flirting aforesaid) very serious-minded, and used to induce Gertie to join all the possible associations for good works. Gertie told us long afterward that Nellie was then very worried about Shelley's doings and made up her mind that Gertie might be able to influence him. Mr Johnson was a minister in a Congregational Church in London and was very much interested in India, even to the extent of learning Hindustani from a Munshi, and when Gertie told him about the Indian girl at College, he asked her to make her acquaintance. So there were many influences urging Gertie towards our family. Gertie made us laugh not long ago by telling us how Nellie, having already joined every possible Good Cause, burst into her room one day at Girton saying: 'We simply must join the Deep Sea Fisherman's League!' This desire to work for and help all good works at the expense of infinite trouble and sacrifice remained with Nellie to the end of her life. After leaving College, Gertie got a post in a private school in Croydon, very near 'Kidderpore', and she and Shelley were constantly thrown together and very soon wanted to get married. But here great difficulties arose. My parents, although they agreed to Nellie's engagement, were most unwilling to have an English daughter-in-law, and her parents even more unwilling for her to marry an Indian, so they were told it was quite out of the question. However, after long opposition and long and weary arguments, all the parents were induced to change their minds. Shelley was called to the Bar in 1893, and in October of that year he and Gertie were married from the Johnsons' house at Hampstead, and after a short honeymoon at Bournemouth sailed for India in the 'Coromandel' for Shelley to begin working at the Calcutta High Court. My father wanted my Mother and all the family to come to Calcutta for Shelley's inauguration as a Barrister, and the time was propitious. Nellie had come down from Girton after getting a good Class II Honours Degree in the Natural Science Tripos and was going to begin her medical studies. Susie had gone up to Newnham in 1891 and would not be able to come at once but would come later, after taking her Tripos in June 1894 with Kali, who would have finished his schooling at Rugby by then and would be going to Oxford. It would not hurt the three younger ones to miss a year of school in England, as they could be sent temporarily to schools in Calcutta, so passages were booked from London to Bombay in the 'Peninsular' in December 1893. But before going on with the narrative I must say something about the wedding.

2.16

Shelley's Wedding
11-10-1893

Mr and Mrs Johnson had six daughters and one son—their youngest child. The eldest, Nellie, had been brilliantly clever, but overstrained her brain, and had a bad mental breakdown from which she never recovered. Gertie was the second, and then came Mary, Minnie, Kitty and Constance, called Cossie, and the boy Ted. Gertie was twenty-three when she was married, just a month older than Shelley. The wedding was in her father's chapel and there were to have been nine bridesmaids, her five sisters and four sisters-in-law, but unfortunately Susie got scarlet fever just before the wedding, so there were eight of us. We wore white ribbed silk frocks and bronze shoes and stockings I fancy, and carried bronze chrysanthemums, as bronze was the 'colour' of Shelley's college. I was much the youngest, and then Milly, as Cossie the youngest sister was considerably older than us. But she was very kind to us children, and I remember thoroughly enjoying the wedding and the fun of spending the night with the Johnsons afterwards. Some days before the wedding there was a large dinner party at Kidderpore, the house being decorated in dark blue and light blue for the Universities, and speeches being made by old family friends all echoing the pious hope that Shelley would follow in his father's footsteps. I remember being much puzzled as to what that phrase actually meant, as my father was so much taller than Shelley!

Before I was six, I had begun going to the kindergarten mentioned before. It was then kept by a Miss Stallybrass and her sister Hilda, and looking back nearly fifty years, it seems to me that it must have been a very good school. We used to play all sorts of Froebel Games, and learn singing and every kind of hand-work—clay modelling, paper-folding, making paper mats, needlework, and manufacturing every kind of contraption in cloth, silk or leather such as hair-tidies, blotting-books, pincushions, etc., which were bestowed on our long-suffering parents as Christmas presents. We were also taught drawing and painting, as well as reading, writing, and elementary arithmetic. From this kindergarten Teenie went on to the Whitgift Grammar School, and I to the High School when I was nearly seven. I always loved school. I can still remember some of the other children at the kindergarten—Lilian Ayworth who was a beautiful child with golden curls and blue eyes, Clement Mason, called 'Chip', Janet Dalziell who was my greatest friend, and Birdie Wilmot, and many others. At the High School I first got to know the Carpenters, whom my parents had known ever since we came to Kidderpore. Dr Carpenter lived very near us at no. 3 Bedford Park, called Wykenham House in memory of his Winchester days. He and his wife were both most delightful people—quite the nicest people I have ever known. His father had also been a doctor, and his mother still lived in Croydon with her only daughter Aimee in a lovely big house near Duppas Hill. There were two older brothers, Evan Carpenter who was an auctioneer and who had a son Rupert, and Edward Carpenter who was a clergyman in Kent and had one daughter Madge. When we first knew Dr Carpenter and his wife they had three little girls, Annie who was two years older than me, and Winnie who was born in 1889. The next year, a week before my brother Kitty died, [another] daughter was born, and I well remember our nurse Lizzie telling us 'Mrs Carpenter has had *another* little girl and she's going to be called 'Barbara Joyce'. When their Uncle Harry, Mrs Carpenter's brother, heard this he said 'What a barbarous choice!' [Our Lizzie's sister, Mary, was the Carpenters' cook for many years—Lizzie left us to get married when we went to India in 1893, and died some few years afterwards of phthisis.] A fifth daughter Doris was born in 1893. I became very fond of all the family, and when my parents went to India in 1900 I was left with them for a year and had a lovely time. There could not have been a greater contrast between the way I was treated by them and the way my elder sisters were treated by the Woods, and I was indeed lucky.

2.17
Visit to India
1893–5

As has already been said, my Mother with Nellie, Milly, Teenie and myself, and a 'sea-going Ayah' sailed for India in early December 1893. I remember George Blair coming to see us off and carrying me up the gangway at Tilbury Docks, getting in front of everybody by saying 'Ladies first, the Bible says so,' and when I was still wondering *where* the Bible said so, he solemnly assured me that I would have to be bathed every day in the foamy water that was pouring out of some hole in the ship's side, and the foam was really soap! We thoroughly enjoyed that voyage, stopping at Gibraltar, Malta, Brindisi, Port Said, Suez, and Aden and going ashore at most of the ports, and getting to Bombay on Christmas Day. My father met us there and we spent a day or two at an hotel called the Apollo Bunder. On the way from Bombay to Calcutta the compartment we were in caught fire, and we had to tumble out and get into another compartment. At Howrah Station, Shelley and Gertie met us and—as the bridge was drawn that day, we had to go across in a boat which added to the excitement.

All the time Teenie and I had been besieging Milly with questions as to what 6 Park Street was like, as she was the only one who remembered it. She told us wonderful tales about the house and all the lovely toys she used to have, and also about a marvellous book she had had there. It was a religious book of some kind, and had three strange pages—one dead black, to show what an unconverted heathen was like; one bright red, for the blood of the lamb; one pure white, for the soul after conversion. I was longing to see this book, and directly we got to the house [*sic*] I ran all over it looking into every cupboard and box I could find, to see if by any chance any of Milly's old toys had been left there, and then begged her to find the book. To my bitter disappointment, although the black and red pages were as described, the white page wasn't pure white at all, but speckled, because the print showed through from the other side!

Satish Mookerjee had been called to the Bar sometime before, and was staying with us as he wanted to go on living in English style. We were all very fond of him. He was very impulsive and affectionate, and adored my mother. He was not as clever as Shelley but very hard working. Unfortunately he never married as at this time he fell deeply in love with a married woman, Mrs P.K. Ray, and remained single all his life for her sake. He had the eastern suite of rooms on the ground floor, and my father the western suite as a dressing room and study. Shelley and Gertie had the first floor eastern suite, and used half of the billiard room as a sitting room and study; my parents had the top center bedroom; Nellie, and Susie, when she came, slept in the east room of the top floor; and Millie and I in the west room; and a small room made from a bit of the verandah was Teenie's room. Thus every room was occupied, and all the stalls were filled, as Nellie, Shelley, Susie and Gertie each had a riding horse; there were two pairs of horses for the barouche and brougham respectively, and a horse for Shelley's landau; and a pony for the three children; and Satish's horse, Rosinante, was also stabled there. The elders had a very gay life, being 'presented' at Government House and taking part in all the gaieties of the season, as well as doing a bit of entertaining in the house.

There were grand ceremonies at Simla House too, for the 'Bowbhat'. Shelley and Gertie and Nellie began at once to learn Bengali with a Pandit, and were soon able to talk a little, Gertie oddly enough getting on much quicker than the others. They learnt Hindustani too, having completely forgotten both languages. So the days were full and enjoyable.

2.18

Life in Calcutta

We younger ones were all sent to school, Milly and myself to the Loreto Convent, and Teenie to St. Xaviers. We thought it very thrilling and romantic to be going to a Roman Catholic Convent, as the Plymouth Brethren spoke in tones of horror of the Church of Rome and used to identify her with the Scarlet Woman in the book of Revelation. We were very happy there, and loved the nuns and only wished we could be Catholics too—at least I did, and so I think did Teenie at St. Xavier's. The Catholic children used to get lovely little lace-edged 'holy pictures' given them, and to go to all sorts of exciting services from which we non-Catholics were debarred. We made a great many friends at the Convent. My chief friends were Probha Sen (now Iyengar), Saraju Gupta (Sen), and Nalini Tagore (Chaudhuri), and among the Anglo-Indian girls—Marie Gasper, Zoe da Cruz, Stella Peters, May Soutar (whose hair was so long that she could sit on it!). Both at school and at home we became very friendly with all of Sir (then Mr) K.G. Gupta's daughters and sons, and the children of Mr R.N. Ray, Monmohun Ghose, Mr P.L. Roy and Dr and Mrs P.K. Ray. We also saw a lot of Lil Palit and used to love spending the day in their enormous house—or rather houses, because Sir Tarak Nath Palit had just built another huge house adjoining his own, for his son Satu who died soon after. We used to go a good deal to Simla House and Bowbazar with my mother, but didn't much like it, and rather despised our cousins for not speaking English, I am ashamed to say! Every morning we used to ride the pony in turn, and in the evenings go for a drive with my mother in the big Barouche. At Easter, we went up to Darjeeling and stayed in an annexe of Woodlands Hotel, then at the height of its prosperity. This was not really our first visit, which should have been mentioned before.

As has been said, my father was very fond of his eldest sister's husband, Satish's father ... [who was a] Government Pleader at Bhagalpur. Unfortunately he got very unwell and developed phthisis, and had to go about to various health resorts. In 1886 he went up to Darjeeling and stayed at Marjorie Villa, and there my mother and father joined him and my Aunt in the autumn, when I was only about three months old. In those days the Cooch Behar houses were not let to people wearing saris, so my aunt had to wear an English dress for the first time. There is a quaint old 'family' group still existing with my aunt in a full skirt and bodice buttoning all down the front, as was then the fashion, my uncle, and their eldest grandson Kalyan aged about eight (he became a doctor and died in a Turkish prison during the great war after the fall of Kut-el-Mara), together with my parents, Kitty, Milly, Teenie and myself. It seems to have been a most successful holiday, and they often talked about it afterwards.

The second visit was also very prosperous, and we were all thrilled with the beauties of Darjeeling. What impressed me most was the Hill Railway and the open compartments with three arms chairs on each side. I do not think there are any left now, as they were most inconvenient in the rains.

My Mother had meant to go back to England in the summer of 1894, but as the first grandchild was expected in November, she decided to stay on to welcome his arrival. In the autumn (pujah holidays), all of us except Shelley and Gertie went up to Mussoorie and had a wonderful holiday there. We stayed at an hotel called 'The Hampton Court Hotel', kept by a Mr and Mrs de Schweppe. I tried to find it many years later, but though I discovered where it had been, it was no longer an hotel. We had some nice picnics and expeditions. I distinctly remember seeing a wonderful conjurer do any number of tricks in the Hotel Gardens—certainly the 'Mango Tree Trick' and, I am almost sure, the 'Rope Trick', but cannot rely upon my memory about this. He was just a casual strolling conjuror and the elders were all out when he came, so only my brother Teenie and myself saw it—or *think* we saw it! I remember especially one delightful picnic to the Kemtie Falls with some friends of my father's called Hersey. One of Captain Hersey's daughters was called Juby, short for Jubilee because she was born in 1887, and we thought it rather unkind to date her like that.

I particularly enjoyed the journey both ways—two nights in the train and then a longer journey from Saharanpur to Dehra Dun and Rojpore, and then eight miles up by Dandy. On the way back, at Allahabad, my mother was amusing herself by bargaining with a Brass merchant for some trays and I was standing by and watching when he suddenly said, 'Memsahib, I will give you all the brass ware in my shop if you will give me that little girl in exchange.' Instead of laughing at him my Mother was terrified, and dropped me into the recesses of the compartment, at which all the others were much amused, and it became a standing family joke!

2.19

Birth of Kew 1894, Return to England 1895

Soon after our return, on 9 November 1894 Shelley's eldest son was born and named Krishto Kumar Edwin Bonnerjee—the Edwin being after Mr Johnson. My parents were delighted with him, and he was a most attractive child and turned out to be an exceptionally clever boy and man. It must have been very hard for Shelley and Gertie to have to begin their married life in the blaze of such publicity, and I often think how much happier everybody would have been afterwards if they had had their own small house and been able to live as they chose. Shelley had been too long away from India to be anything but an alien in his own country. He could never get on with all the relations and Indian friends, nor could Gertie. Their only Indian friends were Basanta Mullick, who afterwards married an English woman, and Rajini Chatterjee and Mrs P.L. Roy.[58] Basanta and his brothers had been great friends of the family at Croydon, when they were students. Otherwise all their friends, interests and ways were English, but here Shelley's nationality prevented complete reciprocity from the English people, and so they were always rather lonely, and isolated to a certain extent. Indians could not join the English Clubs in those days, and there were no Indian Clubs till the Calcutta Club was founded some years later for both English people and Indians, and Shelley later found this a great resort.

I was personally very proud of being an Aunt at the age of eight and adored the new baby. We had a number of old servants at 6 Park Street who had been with my parents for years, and stayed on till they died or were pensioned off. Among these was Lakshmi Ayah, who used to look after me and then was made over to Kew, the Sudder Bearer, Ramjan

Coachman, the old Khausama, and Kumur-ud-din Kitmitgar, some of whom used to come and see us after we were married to get buksis on the strength of having carried us about when we were small.[59]

In April 1895, my parents left for England with Nellie and Susie and the three younger ones in the P&O boat 'Peshawar' from Calcutta to Marseilles. Susie and Kali had arrived in the summer of 1894 on the 'Chusan', and Kali had left after the holidays to go to Oxford. Susie had taken her degree in Natural Science, getting 2nd Class Honours, and both she and Nellie were going to become Medical Students. Nellie was very conscientious, as has already been said, and in the midst of Calcutta gaieties had decided to attend lectures at the Calcutta Medical College in order to waste as little time as possible. Another instance of her conscientiousness was that she induced my father to let her spend the £21 he gave to each of his children on their twenty-first birthdays, in paying for examination fees, as he had already spent so much money upon her education! I think this may partly have been to try to make up for Shelley's extravagances. My father was not particularly pleased, as he could well afford what he spent, but he agreed to her request, although he was much better pleased when Susie spent her present upon buying a gold wrist watch and bracelet—then quite a new form of ornament.

The voyage went well. Milly was then about fourteen and allowed to stay up to dinner, to the great envy of Teenie and myself. She was, as has been said, very pretty and attractive and had many admirers, including the Fifth Officer of the boat who quite 'fell' for her. But as she was constantly with her elder sisters whose cabin she shared, it had to be admiration from a distance! My only sorrow was over the way my mother, whose cabin I shared, used to plait my hair every day to keep it tidy. It was not a loose comfortable 'English' plait beginning at the neck and ending in a loose tail below a broad bow of ribbon, but a real tight 'Indian' plait beginning in the middle of the head, with the ribbon plaited right up to the end and hanging down from there, as this was the only way she knew how to make a plait! In those days one did not argue with one's parents, and after having made a feeble protest and being told this was the best way to keep it tidy in the wind, I just had to put up with the discomfort of a strained-back scalp and 'pulling' hairs until I got used to it! Up till then, I used to have it loose with 'sausage' curls carefully made every day by the nurse or ayah, which was far more comfortable. My chief joy was playing with other children on board—begging, borrowing or stealing long pieces of tape down from the elders and fastening our toy bricks onto these and letting them down into the sea, pretending to fish. We used to spend hours doing this. One man died on board, and there was a funeral at sea which was a tremendous thrill. We children were not supposed to be there of course, but managed to get a very good view from a suitable hiding place. We got to Marseilles in a very high wind which continued all the day while we were sight-seeing, and Susie caught a chill. By the time we got to Paris it turned into acute peritonitis and she was terribly ill, so we delayed a long time there until she got better. Luckily there was a very good doctor and she made a quick recovery, but my parents had an anxious time. We got to Croydon in May. Milly and I began going to the High School under Miss Mullins and there I met several children who are still my friends! Miss Mullins seemed quite old to us then, but when I saw her again in 1933, nearly forty years later, she did not look very much changed, and remembered all about me as a child! Marjorie and Gladys Wilkinson were in the same form as Gwennie Addy, and within the next few years I got to know Phyllis and Marjorie Barnard, Dorothea and Walter Coleridge (twins, and great niece and nephew of Samuel Taylor Coleridge) and renewed my friendship with Annie Carpenter and her sisters. Milly's great friends all the way up the school were Winnie Hinks and Margaret Trinden, now Mrs Reid and Mrs Mallorie.

2.20

Miss Neligan

It is time now to say a little more about the Croydon High School and the first Headmistress, Miss Dorinda Neligan, who was one of our great friends in Croydon.

In the sixties, the condition of Day Schools for Girls in England was most unsatisfactory in every way. The teaching was poor; the standard was very low in the cheaper schools; and in the more expensive schools the classes were usually too small to allow for really efficient teachers to be employed, as it was too expensive to keep a sufficient number. Several ladies interested in the education of girls, including Miss A.J. Clough and Miss Emily Davies, the future principals of Newnham and Girton Colleges, took up the matter and began agitating for the reform of Girls' Education, and as a result a Royal Commission was appointed, and from the report of this Commission, in 1871, Mrs William Grey began a scheme for a National Union for promoting the education of women.[60] The National Union started the Girls' Public Day School Company, and by its means the first High Schools for Girls. These were most excellent schools which are still doing splendid work all over England. The fees were low enough to enable middle class families to send their daughters, and there was a large highly-qualified staff for each school. Croydon High School was opened in 1872 at 'The Chestnuts' North End, but soon moved into its own buildings on Wellesley Road. When I first went to the school there were about three hundred girls. Now there are over 650, and the school has absorbed several of the surrounding houses and their gardens as well as adding on largely to the original buildings, and there is a special kindergarten department at Purley.

The first Headmistress, who was in charge of the school from its opening in 1872 until she resigned in 1902, was Miss Neligan. Since her resignation there have only been two other Headmistresses, Miss Leahy who succeeded Miss Neligan in 1902 and carried on for twenty-five years, and Miss Ransford who is there now.

Extracts from a speech by Miss T. Clark at the Centenary Meeting of Miss Neligan on 28-10-33:

> Miss Neligan was born in Cork (on 13 June 1833). She was the daughter of a soldier, a fact of which she was always proud. Her Mother who was a woman of great culture taught her. She went to Germany and Paris and worked as a 'Finishing Governess'. She was very happy and there is a story of how an old friend of the family proposed to her in the train when she was in tears at leaving her post. She spent her last penny training for the Red Cross during the Franco-German War and went to Metz. The terrible sights and sufferings she saw there filled her with horror, and possibly the seeds of pacifism were sown there.
>
> A typical story of her is told during this period. In the basement of the temporary hospital at Metz there were a large number of desks, but there was no fuel and the men were suffering from the cold. She proposed to use these, but was told that nothing must be touched. Her reply was to send the Orderly for a saw, and she herself sawed up the desks to warm the men.
>
> Miss Neligan had a strong personality, a beautiful Irish voice, a dominating presence and great independence of character. She could work easily with men as few women of her generation could. Her influence permeated the School; to some of the younger children, who did not come much into contact with her, she seemed almost as the God of the Old Testament. They regarded her with awe and dread, but with complete confidence ...
>
> She had keen blue eyes and a look of great authority. She had an Irish sense of humor, so that no story lost anything in her telling. In an age when everybody was easily shocked, Miss Neligan was never shocked. Now, when nobody is shocked, probably she would be. She was a champion of lost causes. In the Boer War she took the unpopular side, and although a prominent member of the constitutional suffrage party, she became a militant suffragist, and it was said she was the only person in the world who could belong to both parties at once!

Another speaker at the same meeting, Mrs Morris, said

> ... coming from a great school under another pioneer Headmistress [Miss Buss of the North London Collegiate School] she was struck by the fact that whenever her former Headmistress looked upon girls rather as potential devils, Miss Neligan tended to treat them as potential angels. At Croydon there were no prizes and practically no rules nor punishments, but the tone of the School was extraordinarily high. It was Miss Neligan's personality that made such a happy state of affairs possible. She was extraordinarily human and marvellously comprehending. She always gave her best and expected their best from others ...

Saturday was always a whole holiday at School, and on Friday mornings there were 'second prayers' at quarter to one and Miss Neligan used to give the whole school a short talk either about politics and world affairs, or on some point of ethics or morals. These talks were impressive and illuminating. A few of the points she was continually bringing before us were: that each individual's aim should be to leave the world, or their own special corner of it at least, a little better for having lived. That money and fame were quite immaterial compared with character. That 'no chain is stronger than its weakest link, no country richer than its poorer, freer than its most oppressed. ...' That the things to remember most were the Fatherhood of God, the brotherhood of man, and to shun *fear*—the cause of most failures. She constantly impressed upon us that women should always be calm and self-possessed and dignified— 'Mistress of herself though China fall' (screaming was a deadly sin in the playground). She had nursed a wounded officer during the Franco-Prussian war whom she had greatly admired (of course the girls suspected a great romance) and she gave each of us a copy of a paper which was found among his things after his death. As it sums up her philosophy of life, I quote it here in full:

Victory

When you are forgotten or neglected or set at nought and you feel resentment, but undiminished love—that is victory!

When your good is evil spoken of, your wishes are crossed, your tastes offended, your advice disregarded, your opinion ridiculed, and you take it all in patient and loving good humour—that is victory!

When you are content in the service of others with any food, any raiment, any climate, any society, any position in life, any solitude, any interruption—that is victory!

When you can, so that the right prevail, truly love to be unknown—that is victory [sic]!'

I have written this full account of Miss Neligan because she was one of the main influences of our lives throughout our Croydon days. She and my father were great friends, as they thought alike about politics, both being liberals and great admirers of Gladstone. Irish and Indian political problems had much in common in those days and there used to be great discussions of all sorts of interesting topics whenever Miss Neligan came to see us.[61] When she resigned the headmistress-ship in 1902, she and her sister Miss Annie Neligan came to stay with us while winding up their affairs and moving to their house on Sydenham Road North; and in our turn we stayed with them much later on when Kidderpore was sold. My father admired her greatly. As has been said, he was always a great advocate of 'Women's Rights'. Dr Garrett Anderson and Mrs Garrett Fawcett were much admired by him, and his ambition was for his daughters to be like them.[62]

2.21

School Days
1895–9

It is very tempting to linger over School Days but as this record is already too long and diffused, I must pass quickly over the next few years, which flowed on prosperously enough. Nellie and Susie attended the School of Medicine for Women and the Royal Free Hospital and finally qualified as doctors in 1899, Susie obtaining the M.B. London degree and Nellie failing to get this, qualified as L.S.A. (Licentiate of the Society of Apothecaries).[63] Kali got his degree from Balliol College Oxford, and then took his Law Exams and was called to the Bar about the same time. Teenie went to Rugby and did well there, and Milly and I went up to the High School prosperously. My father came over every year, sometimes just for the pujah holidays, and sometimes early enough to join us in the summer holidays, which were the only times we went away. In 1896 they were spent at Eastbourne and in 1894 at Swanage, Dorset. That year there was a mania for bicycling, and all the family except myself took to cycling. In 1898 my father came early, and all of us and George Blair and his sister Rotha spent a good holiday ... in the Isle of Skye. In 1899 we went to Eastbourne again, and in December of that year, Nellie and George were married. Shelley and Gertie came over with two children, Kew now five, and Molly, born in February 1899. Gertie had had a bad time, as she lost a small baby who lived only a few days in 1896, and she had great trouble when Molly was born, owing to some slight malformation which increased as she grew older. Molly's head was injured at birth, so that she never became quite normal in intellect. Kew was a charming and very clever child and we all adored him. At the wedding all the family assembled, and this was the last family gathering we were ever to have. Nellie and George were married at the Congregational Chapel in Dingwall Road, Croydon, by George's great friend Mr Pulsford. We three sisters and Rotha Blair were bridesmaids and wore pale yellow crepe de chine frocks and black hats trimmed with yellow, and carried mimosa bouquets. My mother would not leave off her mourning, but wore a very handsome black velvet dress. There was a large reception of all our available friends at Kidderpore, and a grand dinner party that night after the bride and bridegroom had left. The presents were a marvellous sight and filled up the billiard room, as all my father's old friends and 'grateful clients' sent lovely gifts.

Shortly after this wedding Shelley and Gertie left for Calcutta and my father took Susie with him to keep him company, and Kali also went to begin practicing in Madras, under the auspices of Mr Eardley Norton,[64] so the home party was reduced to my mother, Milly and myself, and Teenie in the holidays. The following year, 1900, my father and Susie came over in August, and we met them in Paris and had a Continental Tour. My father engaged a courier—a gentleman called Killerby who wanted to have a holiday on the Continent and could only afford it in this way. He arranged everything for us, and we liked him very much, though he sometimes reduced us to impotent giggling fits by his remarks, which we could not always conceal. We 'did' the Paris Exhibition, and then went to Geneva and all over French and German Switzerland, through the St. Gotthard Tunnel to North Italy, staying a few days at Milan. Then we went to Cologne and up the Rhine to Mainz, to Brussels and Antwerp, and home from Ostend to Dover.

After this wonderful holiday, Milly went off to Newnham College, and as I was the only one permanently at home, my parents decided to leave me with the Carpenters for a year and go back to Calcutta. Nellie and George took a largish house in Liverpool (where George was practising as a barrister on the Northern Circuit) in order to take us all in for the holidays. I was delighted at the idea of staying with the Carpenters, and am ashamed to say that I did not miss my parents and family at all! In fact I rather grudged the time spent at Liverpool, away from my friends, and begged to be allowed to spend the summer holidays with them by the sea instead of going to Nellie's!

I should like to write pages and pages about my stay with the Carpenters of which, even after thirty-six years, I seem to remember every little detail! But it will be enough to say that I was thoroughly happy and loved being one of the elders in a family of five other girls, instead of the youngest at home, with no one very near my age to compare notes with about school affairs. My friends at that time, beside the Carpenters, were the Wilkinsons and Coleridges, the Barnards (with whom I spent several delightful week-ends), Flora Dinn (Mrs Petch) whose brother Hugh was my first 'flame', Gertrude Down (Mrs Le May), Agnes Sterry, Dorothy Stewart (Mrs Reed), Stella Trinder and the Lees, and Lilian and Winnie Scott. I spent the Whitsun weekend with the Sterrys at Redhill, and it was at that house, on a later visit, that I saw a ghost! The incident will be related later on. When I was at the Carpenters, Lil Palit and her mother and brother came over to England and Milly went to stay with them in London and they invited me to spend a day and night and 'do' a theatre. What a thrill that was—an exciting dinner at their house, with strawberries and cream ad lib; then a box for 'The Dandy Fifth' and a grand supper afterwards at (I think) The Criterion, getting home after midnight, and then the fun of going straight to school by train from London, in my best frock and all my friends eager to hear of my experiences!

Mrs Carpenter sometimes took us to London and to the theatre; and when Susie was at home she often took us to Matinees and to museums, picture galleries etc. But usually we lived a very quiet life, as my mother hated going to London and rarely entertained, except for Mothers' Meetings.

2.22

My Father's Retirement and Work at the Privy Council
1902–5

The parents returned in September 1901 and I came back from Corton, Norfolk, where I had been spending the summer holidays with the Carpenters, and we all went up to a place near Glasgow called Kilmalcolm, to see the Glasgow Exhibition. It was a delightful place, and we stayed at a huge Hydro and enjoyed the Turkish Baths there. Here our cousin Benode Gopal, my mother's brother's son, joined us as he had come to England to study for the Bar. He had a very disappointing career and caused my mother much anxiety and sorrow, and we never liked him. My father and Susie went back to Calcutta that winter, but in 1902 they came back to England with Gertie, Kew, Molly and the new baby Nil Kumar Charles, who alas! was a complete invalid. He was a lovely child, with fair hair and blue eyes,—a contrast to Molly who was dark and like my mother. But he was born with some organic trouble, and could never sit up or stand or talk. It was really a release when he died at the age of five, but Gertie of course felt it terribly, and her life must have been most difficult.

My father decided to settle in England and work at the Privy Council and stand for Parliament—his greatest ambition. He had made one attempt in 1898 when he stood as the Liberal Candidate at Barrow-in-Furness, but the Conservative got in. Now he decided to contest the seat for the Walthamstow Division of Essex where the Liberals had a good chance. He got plenty of work at the Privy Council, and Kali, who had come back from Madras, worked as his Secretary, and all would have gone well had his health not begun to fail.[65]

In 1902 we all went for a wonderful tour in Ireland, with Nellie and George. We crossed from Stranaer to Laine (that being the shortest crossing) and went in two jaunting cars all along the coast to the Giant's Causeway. We visited and explored County Donegal, Sligo, and County Galway and stayed at Leename. There to Cork by way of Killarney, and there to Dublin where we spent some time at the Shelbourne Hotel. In 1902 autumn I first met Sara Luce (Mrs Darlington) who came to the High School that year, and she and I became fast friends. She was a Jersey girl, her father being Vicar of St. Saviour's Jersey. She and another friend, Alice Thomson (Mrs Jennings), from Carlisle, came to the High School and stayed in the School Boarding House, nearly opposite our house. Alice came to be a kindergarten student, and was older than we were. As they were both very unhappy at the Boarding House, they spent a great deal of time with us.

Kew was left behind with us for his education, and began going to the High School for Boys, under Mr Hawe as Headmaster. He was brilliantly clever, both then and afterwards, and he made a great success of his life. My mother was devoted to him, and we all loved having him with us.

One good thing resulted from my stay with the Carpenters—I was allowed to continue going to Church with them on Sundays instead of to the Iron Room with my Mother, as I so much preferred it. Susie left off going to the Iron Room and went to St. Michael's Church, near our house, and thus we got to know the Vicar, Canon (then Mr Hoare) and his wife and family, who became great friends of ours. Susie often used to take me to Church with her, and I always liked it, as much as I disliked the Iron Room. She was baptised and confirmed at St. Michael's Church. My father did not much like it, but as she was over twenty-one, and allowed to please herself. When I wanted to be baptised, he refused his consent as I was under twenty-one. After a few years, I decided to be baptised whether he agreed or no, so with the support of my mother and Susie, I was baptised and confirmed when I was eighteen. My father was not told officially, but of course he knew all about it unofficially and did not really seem to mind, as he had vindicated his opinion by refusing consent! We were the only members of the family who were baptised. Nellie had desired it at one time, but changed her mind before she was twenty-one.

In the summer of 1903 we took a house at Harlyn Bay near Padstow Cornwall, and had a very pleasant holiday with all the family and many guests—including Miss Neligan, and Susie's great friends and old fellow-student Dr Christine Murrell, who became famous in later years as a pioneer among Medical Women. But though it seemed such a successful holiday, my father, as we heard later, then first began to be aware of ominous swelling of the ankles and feet and other signs of kidney trouble. He went on with his most congenial work and political activities for the next two years, but became increasingly unwell.

Milly came down from Newnham in 1903 after taking an Honours Degree in Classics, and spent a year studying at the Sorbonne in Paris. Susie decided to take up medical work in earnest, and joined the Cambridge Mission to Delhi at the end of 1903. She liked the work and became great friends with the head doctor there, Dr Muller. But in the summer of 1905, hearing of my father's increasing ill-health, she thought it her duty to come home and nurse him. His eyesight was rapidly failing and he was getting severe heart-attacks. The summer of 1904 we spent at Llandudno in North Wales, and the spring of 1905 at St. Leonards-on-Sea—nothing did my father much good. Kali had come home from Madras as has been said, and helped him as his Secretary, but at the beginning of 1906 he had to give up both work and politics and live an invalid's life. This was a crushing blow, as he had had great success at Walthamstow, and when the Liberal Candidate who succeeded him did get elected at the General Election of 1906, he felt that if only he could have continued there, he would have achieved his life's ambition. This last year of his life was one of many disappointments. He was very much worried over Indian politics, and did not know what to feel about 'Young India' and other Partition agitation. His great friend Mr Raj Narayan Mitter came to England in 1905 with cancer of the throat and made his headquarters with us. As the London doctors could do nothing, he went to Germany to be operated upon by a surgeon there who had pronounced the only chance of cure to be an operation—feasible but risky. Susie went with him to Berlin, but he died under the anesthetic. She had a very difficult time arranging for his cremation, cabling his wife and family, and having to go through all the German formalities before she could collect and pack the ashes and despatch to Calcutta according to his wife's instructions—and all without knowing a word of the language! My father had been told that Professor Pagenstecher of Wiesbaden was a wonderful eye specialist and decided to go to him for treatment; so Susie went from Berlin to Wiesbaden where my parents, Milly and myself joined her, and both my father and my mother, who were suffering from glaucoma, went to Dr Pagenstecher's clinic.

2.23

College Days
1904–7

In the meantime I had been going on with my school work, and passed all my exams successfully—Junior Cambridge in 1901, London Matriculation in 1902, Higher Certificate in 1903, Higher Local and ... Cambridge University Entrance [exams] in 1904, winning a school scholarship of £15 but failing to get a scholarship at Newnham. In the autumn of 1904 I went up to Newnham and took Natural Science, Chemistry, Zoology and Physiology. I am tempted to write pages and pages about my college days, but as the history of higher education for women and their struggle to get degrees, and also the history of Newnham College, has been fully described many times, I must refrain. I loved all my three years at college—the delight of being 'on one's own' and meeting all sorts of new and exciting friends; the lovely gardens at college, the expeditions around Cambridge; the fun of being able to specialize and work in well-equipped laboratories after the makeshifts we had at school (though modern students would not think our laboratories of 1904 well-equipped!)—all these were perpetual pleasures. The friends I made there are still my great friends now—Audrey Addison from London, Margaret Butler (Mrs Western) from Weybridge, Margery Beverly from Norwich, Eleanor Welch (Mrs Lee) from Birmingham, Eleanor Walrond and Dorothy Chamberlain from Rugby, Elinor Lupton from Leeds, Mary Fyffe (Mrs Picton Turbervile) from Horsham Sussex, Muriel Virgo from London, Florence Banbridge ... from Barnsley and many others—and how much I used to enjoy going to stay with them in the holidays, as I often did. Of course I was very much worried about my father, but did not then realize how very serious his illness was, and would forget about it at times.

In the Easter of 1906 the family went to Falmouth, as a sort of forlorn hope that the change might do my father some good, and I joined them there after a most enjoyable Reading Party with Mary Fyffe, Dorothy Chamberlain and Elsie Collier at Dallington, Sussex.

On our return from Wiesbaden in the autumn of 1906, Milly became engaged to Omi Chaudhuri whom she had known a little at Cambridge, and met again at Ida Ghose's. My father consented to the engagement though he never seemed anxious that his daughters should marry and would rather have seen them established in professions! He knew the family well, as the eldest brother Sir Ashutosh was a friend of his, and two of the other brothers, Kumood and Pramatha, used to come and see us very often at Croydon when we were students in the 'nineties. My mother was very pleased, as she wanted her daughters to get married. Milly had had many 'suitors' but would never look at any of them; and Susie and I had had many dreary an afternoon trying to entertain one very persistent one—a Dr Bhattacharya, whose suit my mother rather favoured, but of whom Milly did not approve. She made a league with our parlour maid Florence to give her a chance to escape (out of the back door if necessary) whenever he came to call! She used to manage this so secretly that Susie and I, fully thinking she was at home and would appear at any moment, used to make conversation with the unfortunate doctor till Florence, bringing in tea, would firmly announce that Miss Milly had gone out long ago!

Nellie and George came down to stay with us at Falmouth and also Mr Jyotish Ghose (Sir Chunder Madhub Ghose's grandson, whose guardian my father was during his student days, and whom my father always called 'Mr Astrologer'). We saw a great deal of him and found him a most curious individual. It was at Falmouth that George had his first violent attacks of gallstones, and after that he had to have continual operations and never recovered his health.

2.24

Death of W.C. Bonnerjee
21-7-06

Falmouth could not do my father any good, so the family went back to Croydon, and there he steadily grew worse. I went back to Cambridge after the holidays, and went up again for the long vacation in July, but was hastily summoned home on the 20th, and he died on Saturday, 21 July, in the evening. The funeral was on the 25th at Golders Green Crematorium, and a large number of friends came to it. According to his express wish there was no religious ceremony at all, but Mr Gokhale[66] (who, with Mr R.C. Dutt, had been coming to Croydon every day during that sad time and giving us great comfort and support, as also did Miss Neligan) made a speech. Amongst other things he said:

> Mr Bonnerjee was an ardent patriot, a wise and far-sighted leader, an incessant worker, a man whose nobility of mind and greatness of soul were stamped on every utterance of his life. His intellectual gifts were of the very highest order. Endowed with an intellect at once critical, vigorous and comprehensive, a truly marvellous memory, luminous powers of exposition, captivating eloquence, great industry and a wonderful habit of method and discipline, he was bound to achieve, in whatever field he chose to work brilliant success. He had a wide outlook on life, deep and earnest feelings, and a passionate desire to devote his great gifts to the service of his country. And added to these was that combination of strength and restraint which made him one of the most manly men that one could come across. Such a man must tower above his fellowmen wherever he was placed. In a self-governing country he would, without doubt, have attained the position of a Prime Minister. Till the moment of his death Mr Bonnerjee (with two or

three others) was the very life and soul of the Congress movement. He ungrudgingly gave to its cause his time and his resources, and this far more than is generally known. He cheerfully bore all its anxieties, his exertions for its success were unwearied, and no man's counsel was valued higher by his countrymen where the Congress was concerned. His courage was splendid, and it rose with difficulties, and his nerve and his clear judgment were a theme of constant admiration among his countrymen. With Mr Bonnerjee at the helm, everyone felt safe. His was the eloquence that thrills and steers and inspires, but his was also the practical sagacity that sees the difference between what may be attained and what cannot, and when the need arose no man was firmer than Mr Bonnerjee in exercising a sobering and restraining influence.

My mother and all of us went to the funeral, and were comforted and cheered by Mr Gokhale's words, and all the tokens of admiration and grief from all the friends there. Some days later, and again according to his wish, the ashes were buried in my brother's grave at Croydon cemetery and the following epitaph, dictated to Susie the day before he died by my father himself, was engraved upon the tombstone: 'Here beside the ashes of his son rest the ashes of Womesh Chunder Bonnerjee Hindu Brahmin who died on a visit to England [and] fell a victim to Bright's Disease on 21-7-06,' and to these words were added the verse from Acts 13:36: '[He] after he had served his own generation by the will of God fell on sleep.'

He wanted to die in his own country, and the last few days of his life, when he was wandering in mind a good deal, he kept on telling my mother that they must pack up and start for India immediately—this explains the 'while on a visit to England'.

Meetings were held in India in his memory, and a short ceremony was held at the High Court Calcutta on 23 July when the acting Chief Justice (Sir Chunder Madhub Ghose) and Lord Sinha and others made speeches about him. My mother was well-nigh inundated with letters and telegrams, and there were so many references to my father in the Indian and English papers that we had to employ a Press Cutting Agency to collect them.

My poor Mother! Her state of mind can better be imagined than described, and her grief, though for the most part silent, was so intense that no one knew how to begin to comfort her. But she did not give way, as when her son died; she was brave and strong and did everything she was told for his sake. Her religion was her only comfort, and her simple almost child-like faith in God's love and mercy held her up in this overwhelming tragedy, when she had, for the first time, to stand alone without her husband's aid.

She found herself plunged, for the remainder of her life, in a sea of business and other worries, as the heir to my father's money. Instead of leaving her only a life interest in his property, he left everything to her, to be divided equally among the children after her death unless she choose to alter this division. I think he hoped by this means to keep all her children attached to her, as she would be the sole arbiter of the amount of their inheritance. But it landed her in endless business problems. The Executor was my Father's clerk (and cousin) Babu Baney Madhub Mookerjee. This appointment was made by my father to save Shelley trouble, but he was much hurt by what he considered was a token of mistrust in him, and fancied Susie and others had been influencing my father against him which was so far from being the case that Susie had warned my father how Shelley would feel about it.

2.25

Remaining Years of Hemangini Bonnerjee's Life
1906–10

At the beginning of 1907, Susie and Milly went to Calcutta, at Susie's suggestion. She wanted to set up a practice there, and felt Milly's marriage ought to take place fairly soon and that she should have a chance of meeting her future relations. Gertie had come to England the previous summer to deposit Molly with her mother, to be taught by her Aunt Minnie, and was there when my father died, and joined us in a short stay at Ilfracombe in September, as we hoped a change might do Mother good. Gertie had left the invalid child, now five years old, with his nurse and his father, and when she got back to Bombay she was met with the news of his death. Though it was a real release, it upset her terribly, particularly as she had not been there at the time. Shelley and she let the top flat of 6 Park Street—without telling my mother—to a couple of young English men. This was only discovered when Susie and Milly got to Calcutta the following January and my mother was terribly upset and grieved about it. It seemed to her a sort of sacrilege that any part of my father's house should be let to strangers. Gertie's excuse was that she could not bear to have an empty nursery upstairs. This behavior, and Shelley's annoyance at the appointment of the Executor of the will, caused a coolness between them and the rest of the family, of which Susie was to bear the brunt. They did not help her in her endeavours to find a suitable place for a Surgery, or to get a post in Calcutta, and finally she decided to go back to her Delhi work again. In the summer I came down from Cambridge after taking my Honours degree in Natural

Science; Omi, had gone to Balliol College, Oxford, in 1903, and then after taking his degree there in Honours, had been called to the Bar in 1904 was going to practice in Calcutta; and Kali had gone a few months earlier to Rangoon to practice there. So my mother decided to go to Calcutta with Teenie and myself for Milly's marriage. We left in June on the 'Somali' from London to Calcutta. That voyage was a very sad time for her, with so many memories of former happy voyages; and the arrival in Calcutta without my father to meet her was almost more than she could bear. But she was very brave, for our sakes, and felt she was doing what he would have wished, as he particularly told her she must be at Milly's wedding. To Teenie and myself it was very exciting, as we remembered a little about Calcutta and the lovely house. Milly was married on 13 August 1907 at 6 Park Street, and she and Omi took a house at 9 Queens Park, Ballygunge, while their own house at 42 Jhowtala was being built. My mother grew fond of Omi, and was very happy about Milly. Teenie got engaged to Amiya Roy (Kitty), a daughter of the late Mr R.N. Roy, who had been a friend of my father, and was married to her on 2 October 1904. Susie came back to Calcutta from Delhi as she was not keeping well there. Shelley and Gertie were still much estranged from the rest of the family, though still living in the same house, and my mother felt very sad about this. She and Susie and I sailed for England once more in November on the S.S. Nubia, leaving Teenie and his wife established in the top flat, and Shelley and Gertie in the rest of the house at 6 Park Street. Back in England we decided to sell 'Kidderpore' Croydon as it was far too big for our reduced numbers. While a purchaser was being found, I began my teacher's training course at the London Day Training College, and also did voluntary work at the Charity Organisation Society's Newington Branch and Susie took up research work in Cambridge as Assistant to a Dr Strangeways. My father's eldest sister's grandson Kalyan Mookerjee, now a doctor, came to live with us for a time, to take the D.P.H. degree, and later went to Nellie and George at Liverpool; and Dhiren Ghose (brother of Sir C.C. Ghose) stayed in a boarding house near us to be under my mother's guardianship at the earnest request of his brother, though she was very unwilling to take responsibility. So we saw a lot of these young men, and of my old school and college friends, and I personally was very busy and happy that last year in Croydon, except for watching my mother's grief.

At last 'Kidderpore' was sold to the present owners, to be an orphanage for army officers' daughters, and we decided to settle in London, somewhere near Regents' Park. But in the meantime, Milly's eldest son, Joyanta (Muchu), had been born on 10 June 1908 and my mother was very anxious to see him, as she had always adored babies. Kew had gone to a preparatory (boarding) school for Rugby called Bilton Grange in 1906, and could spend his holiday with his other grandmother at Hampstead. So my mother and I set off once more for Calcutta in October '08 on the 'Caledonia', our last weeks in Croydon being spent with Miss Neligan and her sister. When we got to Colombo, we had a cable to say that Teenie's eldest son Bharat had been born on 26 October, so the prospect of two grandsons to greet her cheered my mother very much. She took over charge of Bharat on our arrival, and he was her great resource during this, the last year of her life. Shelley and Gertie had decided to move to a house of their own, and were first at 12 Rawden Street and then at 1 Ballygunge Park. They were sorry about the coolness between them and my mother, and used to come to see her again, and she was very glad to welcome them, though things could never be as before.

Teenie met P.K.M. at the Bar Library and became friendly with him in the winter of 1908–9 and one Sunday in December he came with Lil Palit to tea and tennis at 6 Park Street and we met for the first time. After this we met fairly frequently, being 'thrown together' by Lil, and the result was that we got engaged to be married in the April of 1909. My mother was not keeping at all well at this time, and suffered constantly from dyspepsia. After my father's death, she gave up meat, fish, and eggs (a sort of reversion to her old Hindu ideas) and we felt that this upset her digestion. She was still perpetually worried with business matters and decisions, and seemed to feel my father's absence more and more. But she did have gleams of happiness, in the grandsons, and in spending long days with the sisters-in-law and talking over old times, and in the devotion felt for her by them and by their children and grandchildren. All father's sisters' sons—Satish (who had never married because of his devotion to Mrs P.K. Ray), Suresh, Bishu, Bhubon, Debar, Noni and Jyoti used to come to see her every week and she took great pleasure in their company, and that of her stepsister and her family, now [that she was] a widow. Her mother had died as lately as 1906, just a month after my father. And during all this time of pain and sickness and failing eyesight—for she could barely see to write and knit, and not at all to read except the very largest of print—her religion held her up. She enjoyed knitting especially, and could just see enough to play cards, so we constantly played bridge and bezique with her to keep her mind from worrying. She was very fond of Omi, and was very thankful that my future was provided for. In the autumn she and Kitty and Bharat and I went to Shillong for a month or so, but her health rapidly deteriorated. I was married on 26 November, and P.M. and I went to Barrackpore for our honeymoon and then went to live at 66 Lower Circular Road. We had to be married in the Scotch Church as he was not a Christian, and under the act which provides for the marriage of a Christian and a non-Christian. There was a very grand reception at 6 Park Street. We drove back from Church in a carriage with an English coachman and groom hired for the occasion from Cook's, which caused a great sensation! We motored down to Barrackpore in an Argyll car lent to us for the honeymoon by Mr N.C. Mallick, and as cars were still quite new in those days, we felt very superior. We also had a trap and pony, and P.M. taught me to drive both the pony and the car. He had already taught me to ride during our engagement, and gave me a white horse called 'Chance' as his first present to me! At the wedding I wore a white crepe de chine dress with a silver panel down the front, and silver shoes and stockings and a long net veil with orange blossom; and for going away I had a mauve crepe dress trimmed with string-coloured lace, and a mauve 'motor bonnet' and a tussore dust coat piped in black. The trousseau was really lovely, chosen by Susie in England, and made by our old Croydon dressmaker Mrs Hackett. There were 12 sets of everything, and those frilled petticoats and cambric night gowns make one smile to think of now, so elaborately were they trimmed with rows and rows of insertion and lace. I remember with pleasure the coloured silk stockings and shoes to match all the frocks!

But I scarcely wore the frocks. My mother's health grew worse and worse and at last the doctor discovered an intestinal growth to be the cause of all her suffering. She was operated upon on 3 January and died on 7 January, conscious up to the end, and so very thankful to be going to join her husband, as she said. I shall never forget her look of intense joy when the doctors thought it right to warn her that she had only a few hours to live. She was, as ever, far more thoughtful about the comforts of her children and nurses than about her own pain, and kept urging us to rest, and go down for meals. She died bravely and gladly, as one really 'Going Home'.

She was buried on 8 January in the Calcutta Cemetery, and we put on her tombstone, as summing up her life of brave faith: 'I have fought a good fight, I have finished my course, I have kept the faith.'

Part 3

Early Married Life[67]

3.1

6 Park Street Again
1908

Before beginning an account of my early married life, I must go back a little to say that although the last two years of my mother's life were so sad and dreary for her, the youngest members of the family managed to get a good deal of pleasure for themselves, apart from sympathizing with, and doing all they could to help her. Personally I much enjoyed Calcutta life, and meeting so many new and very old friends. We renewed our friendship with the B.L. Gupta family whom we had met in England, and Lulu who was my age became a great friend. Omi Chaudhuri's mother and relations were all exceedingly kind and hospitable to us, and accepted me as one of the family for Milly's sake and I went to many pleasant parties at Sir A. Chaudhuri's (Omi's eldest brother's) magnificent house at Ballygunge. Kitty's family were also very friendly; Teenie and Kitty called upon the Judges' wives and other Calcutta people and did a lot of entertaining and took me wherever they went. The Calcutta Ladies Branch of the National Indian Association had just been opened in Calcutta, and there we met a great many English ladies who have since become lifelong friends—Lady Holmwood, Lady Stephen, Mrs Dural, Mrs Bompas, Lady Stuart, Violet Clinton Baker, Mrs Keays, Mrs Bear, Lady Monteath and many others. Parties were given once a month by the various members in their own houses or gardens, and as the membership then was small and select we used to enjoy them. I became joint Honorary Secretary of the Association, and kept this office for eight or nine years. Every Sunday there were tennis parties at 6 Park Street, and Kitty was one of the most delightful hostesses I have ever come across. Teenie was also a wonderful host, and he has always had an exceptional faculty for making friends, so a great many interesting people used to come to the house, both Indian and English. ... Amongst these were Mr B.G. Horniman, then of the *Statesman* staff, and his friend Douglas Humphries, who were called 'the white babus' for their Indian sympathies. Mr Humphries died young but Mr Horniman is still in India, at Bombay, and still works for Indian freedom.

After my engagement P.M. taught me to ride, and we were to go out riding every morning which was a wonderful experience for me. In the evenings he used to call for me and take me out for a drive in his high dog cart and then come back to dinner. He also bought a nice little car, and we used to go out in that to visit the various relations. I also used to have Bengali lessons every morning for an hour—with homework! Thus the days passed very quickly, though of course my mother's grief and suffering cast a shadow over everything, in spite of her brave patience. She always encouraged us to go about as much as possible and to entertain our friends, and she used to like meeting her old friends and, most of all, spending long days with her sisters-in-law and talking about my father. She missed her 'Meetings' very much, and used to go to the Scottish Church in Wellesley Street, though sometimes she would come with me to St. James' Church which I used to attend regularly. The Chaplain then was Canon Smith, who afterwards became a friend of ours.

3.2

Early Married Life
1909–10

As has been said, our first house after our marriage was no. 66 Lower Circular Road, up a lane almost opposite St. James' Church. The approach was bad and the neighbourhood somewhat slummy, but the house itself was quite liveable (a cousin of mine [Kalyan's mother] called the house 'a lotus on a dungheap'!). It was two storied with two rooms on each floor; the downstairs rooms were rather damp but could be used as dining room and dressing room, and there was a tiny office room and a verandah. Upstairs there was a drawing room and bedroom and a long verandah with a tin roof, which was too hot to be used in the summer though pleasant enough in winter, and a small open balcony facing south which was a great resort in summer evening. We had a pony called 'Baby Boy' and a trap, and also the small brougham from 6 Park Street, but this was not very useful at first, as we had no coachman! We began life on about Rs 325 a month but soon after we were married, P.M. was appointed Receiver of the Paikpara Estate, and that brought in some more money.

We lived very quietly indeed the whole of that first year, as my mother died in January of 1910, and soon after that I was very unwell and had to lie flat on my back from the middle of April till the end of June. We refused all invitations at first, but we had one little 'outing' before my illness. This was to Chapra, Behar, on some Paikpara business, and we had to spend several hours at Bankipore on the way, and were able to drive round the town, which later was transformed into Patna, and we saw the huge granary built by Warren Hastings, which has such a curious echo. At Chapra we met Babu Bansidhar Gupta (whose daughter married P.M.'s eldest sister's second son) and various other family connections. This was my first experience of real dry heat which chapped and blistered the skin as never happens in Calcutta. Once when P.M. went to Islampur for a wedding I went to spend a few days with Milly at Jhowtala, their newly built house, which then had only 6 rooms, 3 upstairs and 3 downstairs, and enjoyed their lovely garden and country aspect. One day Ida Ghose came to see us at no. 66 and brought Buddhi Gupta with her. Buddhi had married Romesh Gupta in April 1910 and this was our first meeting.

Kitty and Teenie had moved into a flat on Theatre Road after my mother's death. We had found that it would be better to sell 6 Park Street as no member of the family could afford to keep such a large establishment, and it was bought by a Marwari merchant and let out in flats. The house (now no. 24) is still there, but the garden was acquired by a motor car firm and a large garage built facing the street so the house is no longer visible from the road ... [illegible] ... The neigbourhood also has completely changed from a residential area into a very busy shopping centre, and none of us have ever regretted the sale of no. 6.

After several months of ill health on my part, Tara was born on 6 September 1910. Dr Rachel Cohen, Superintendent of the Dufferin Hospital, whom Nellie had first met when she began studying at the Medical College in 1894, looked after me, and Milly was also there and had the new born baby almost thrown into her arms by Dr Cohen, somewhat to her embarrassment! P.M.'s eldest nephew Tom was also staying with us, en route for Puri, where he took up the post of Superintendent of the Paikpara Estate and worked there for a good many years. Pinu was also in Calcutta studying for the B.A. and B.L. examination, and he often used to come and see us, and P.M.'s mother and sisters used to come whenever they were passing through Calcutta and were always exceedingly kind and friendly. It must have been a great blow to them all when the only surviving son married out of caste, but they never let it make any difference to their affection and always welcomed me as a member of the family, in spite of my different religion, upbringing and general outlook. This was all the more surprising, as village-dwelling families are always more orthodox and set in their ways than town dwellers, and no other member of the family had ever dreamed of breaking off from orthodox Hinduism—nor have they up to this day!

With Tara's birth, no. 66 Lower Circular Road became too small for us, and we began to look about for a larger house. We were lucky to find one in no. 1 Elysium Row, the nicest part of Calcutta, just beyond the Cathedral, and a few minutes walk from the *maidan*. This was what is called a 'demi-upper-storey' house—really two-storied, but the lower rooms were too low to use much. P.M. made one of them into a dressingroom, and two others into an office and waiting rooms. Upstairs, there were three nice-sized bedrooms, a drawing room, sitting room, dining room and pantry, and a long narrow south veranda where we lived all the summer months. There was no proper garden, except for a narrow strip on the south and east, and an imposing portico with an open verandah above it. But to the west there were five stalls for horses, and a huge coach house, where we used to keep two carriages and a car.

We spent a month in Milly's ever-hospitable house while they were away in Hazaribagh, and no. 1 Elysium was being repaired and repainted, and moved in in November 1901. We were very comfortable there, and eventually managed to purchase the house, but sold it in 1919, when we built a house in Ballygunge and a house at Alipore during the post-war boom in house property.

3.3

Life at Elysium Row

During the next few years, the families increased rapidly. Minnie Bonnerjee was born in March 1911, Dilip Chaudhuri in August 1911, and Jai Krishna Majumdar in December 1911 ... . In 1912, on 10 September, Anil Chaudhuri was born, and that autumn we shared 'La Roche' Darjeeling with the Chaudhuris, having between us six children under 5! I remember being impressed with Milly's unfailing accuracy in pronouncing *which* child was crying when wails were heard! That same summer Kitty had gone to England for the first time with Bharat, Protep (*b*. 5-2-1910), and Minnie, aged respectively 3, 2 and 1!

Susie had left Calcutta shortly after my mother's death, and after working for a further period at Cambridge with Dr Strangeways, took a nice house in Ealing and furnished it sumptuously, intending to take in Indian students as paying guests. It was to this house that Kitty went with the children, and as Susie had just hired a roomy motor car and chauffeur, they had a pleasant stay. Teenie joined them in pujah holidays and they all came back together in November, to no. 11 Ballygunge Circular Road ... [bringing] with them a very nice English Nanny, Rose Wright.

In 1913, Sheila Bonnerjee was born on 24 June and Karun Majumdar on 6 September. Amita Chaudhuri arrived on 16 November 1915, and Eileen (Anile) Bonnerjee and Indira Bonnerjee on 14 January 1916 and 11 April 1918 respectively, thus completing the families ... . Jai first rode a pony in Darjeeling before he was a year old ... they had their own ponies and used to come out with us. They also had a tiny goat-carriage drawn by a huge black goat called Pam. We bought a Phaeton, and a nice grey horse for it called Philip (after Mr Phillip Gray, a friend of

Teenie's) and the children went for a drive in this every evening. We also had a Chenard Walker car, and later on bought a very convenient two-seater Clement Talbot in which P.M. and I used to go for evening drives.

In 1914 the War broke out, and although we did not really feel it much at first in India, it was an anxious time, and we all did a good deal of War work—knitting mufflers and socks, and packing parcels for the Indian troops in East Africa and Mesopotamia. The National Indian Association[63] opened a War Work Depot and we used to go there once a week, or oftener, to pack 'gur' and 'dantons' and kurtas for the troops, and roll bandages and make pneumonia-jackets, etc. We also used to visit the Alipore Garrison Hospital and do what we could for the soldiers there.

At the same time there was the children's early schooling to be thought of. At first we were much impressed with the Montessori Method, and I had a lot of the apparatus made by Monsieur Martin, the kindly manager of the French Motor Company. The children seemed to do everything far too quickly (bad teaching, I now suspect) and then play 'trains' with the pieces! But I taught them to write English very quickly in the Montessori way, by feeling letters made of emery paper. Tara learnt to read out of a very old fashioned book which I had had as a child called *Reading without Tears*, but I taught Jai on the 'Nelly Dale' System. Tara became an accurate speller without difficulty, but Jai could never learn to spell, and I am not sure whether this was due to concentration or method! They also had lessons in Bengali every day from a girl trained at Miss Ryson's School until they went to school.

But life was not entirely domestic. Both Milly and I joined various Associations, including the Association for British University Women in India, which used to meet once a month and have lectures and discussions. This Association was founded by Lady Stephens, who had been at Girton as Miss Shaw Nightingale and was a cousin of Florence Nightingale. Her sister-in-law Miss Stephen was Vice-Principal of Sidgwick Hall at Newnham when I was there, and was later Principal of Newnham College.[69] Her husband Sir Harry was a High Court Judge. She amused us by saying, when she founded this Association, that it was so important that educated women should 'find each other out'! Then we had to join the Graduates' Union, for graduates of all universities, which also entailed monthly meetings at the Y.W.C.A. Institute. We also joined a Browning Society, of which Mrs Bear and Mrs Keays were keen members, and six or seven of us used to meet once a week and read and try to understand the less well-known poems. ... We also used to meet a few select souls at Mr Percy Brown's house in the evenings, once a week or so, to read Greek plays—in translation of course. I also joined the Oxford Mission Association, which arranged for short Missionary Services in a different church of the town every month, preceded by tea at the chaplain's house. It was most interesting meeting the Oxford Mission Fathers and the Sisters, and also getting to know the various chaplains; P.M. and I often used to go visit Father Douglass at Behala, taking the children with us. I was also asked to join a Ladies' Bible Class, conducted by Mrs Sandys, held once a week at Mrs Haskell's in Elysium Row, and joined the Mothers' Union in 1915. So what with early morning rides, looking after and teaching the children in the mornings, various Association meetings in the afternoon, and evening drives with P.M., and friends' tea parties and N.I.A. parties and other social functions the days were quite full. The only breaks in our life were the annual pujah holidays, when we usually went to Darjeeling, taking a house for a few months or so and thinking how wonderful it would be to possess a house of our own there. In 1915 we went to Mussoorie, and in 1918 to Simultala; otherwise we went regularly to Darjeeling from 1911 to 1920, when we left Calcutta for good.

3.4

Visits of Nellie and Susie to India

As has been already told, after their marriage in 1899, Nellie and George settled in Liverpool, where George joined the Northern Circuit and also worked hard with the Liverpool Scottish Territorial Regiment where he rapidly became a Major. Nellie did such medical works as came her way, and also a great deal of social work for the Baby Clinics, etc., visiting the School for the Blind, and working hard for the Indian Famine Fund Union, Liverpool Branch, for which she used to arrange meetings and speakers, and collect money. She also did anything she could for any Indian students who came her way, deserving or undeserving, and her great wish was to work for India always. When Kalyan Mukherjee went to England in 1904 he had to do some work in Liverpool and stayed with her and she became very fond of him. Later on, his brother Kusal went to England to study art, and stayed with her for seven years and she was truly delighted to have him with her. After a year or so in Liverpool, they moved out first to Waterloo and then to Formby. After Mr Blair's death, Mrs Blair settled in Southport and remained there till she died in 1922. This was very convenient for George, as Southport is very near Formby and he could constantly be with his mother.

Nellie had certain investments in India, and as these required personal attention she decided to come to Calcutta on a short visit in 1911, leaving George to look after, and be looked after, by his mother, as his health continued to be very bad after those first attacks in 1906. She arrived in June 1911 and stayed part of the time with Milly and part of the time with us. She was really delighted to be in India again, after sixteen years, and gave our relations great pleasure by spending several weekends at Simla House. She seemed to find no difficulties in adapting herself to Indian ways of living and Indian food! Milly had begun wearing a sari and discarded English dress altogether immediately after her marriage, and I followed her example after Tara's birth. Seeing us both in saris Nellie longed to wear them too, and took some away with her when she left, hoping George would allow her to wear them—which he did. I should have mentioned before that my father always insisted upon our wearing English dress and would never allow us to put on saris, even for fun. This was, I imagine, because of the disrepute sari-wearing women had been in forty years earlier, if they went about, and he retained this early prejudice as long as he lived.

Nellie was always a very healthy woman, in spite of her untiring energy, and what illnesses she ever had were through accidents. A few years after her marriage, when they first moved to Waterloo (a suburb of Liverpool) she was alone in the house and was cooking one day when in bending over the fire a celluloid comb in her hair caught fire and rapidly set her hair alight. She managed to extinguish the flames, to telephone a doctor friend, and open the front door before she collapsed. The burns were terrible and it took her a long time to get over them, and the scars remained till the day of her death. As all her hair was burnt off and the scalp badly injured, she had to wear a wig for many years. Another time she broke her right wrist in an accident when a heavy weight fell on it—during a removal from one house to another. Yet another time, when doing some microscope work, she injured her eyes from using too bright a light unshaded.

It was pleasant seeing her again, though her visit was very short, lasting only from July to September 1911—and we younger members of the family were rather alarmed by her ceaseless energy and longing to work for others, whether they wanted her services and appreciated them or not; and most of all by her thinking that we ought to work too!

As has been said, Susie hoped to take Indian students in her Ealing house, and she did have one paying guest, Mr Ram Maulik, who was a connection of our cousin Deveswar Mookerjee. But she was not the right person to keep a boarding house, and the attempt was a failure. When the War broke out, she took in a number of Belgian refugees, but soon afterwards her servants wanted to leave her to take up work in a Munitions factory, and she found it so hard to get other maids that she decided to give up the house, store the furniture and come to India on a visit. She arrived in January 1915 and spent three months in Calcutta staying in turn with Milly, Teenie and myself. She was, I think, really pleased to see us again and was very good to us, though not a very easy guest as she was often critical. I was strongly reminded of her when, reading [a biography of] ... Mrs Henry Fawcett, as though the following words might have been written for her: 'She was perhaps a little formidable to the young ones, for she never let things slip by or tried to hide a disapproval she felt; yet she was endlessly kind, and always willing to take trouble for them, and so truly sympathetic that even her reproofs were welcomed, and her approbation valued more than that of anyone else.'[70] Like Nellie, she was full of untiring energy, but unlike her she was very delicate and suffered terribly from insomnia and dyspepsia, and took far too many medicines to try to cure these. The insomnia began as a result of her medical work in Delhi in 1904. She was the only doctor in the Mission Station at Karnal during a severe plague epidemic and was continually called up at night, and could not sleep in the intervals. Then, during my father's long decline she had to be on the watch for sudden heart attacks and be ready to administer oxygen at any time of the day or night, and thus insomnia became a habit she could never get rid of. She was passionately fond of dogs, and always kept one or more, all her life, and when she came to India this time she had a delightful bull dog called Benjy with her. She went back again in March 1915, but came back again in the winter of 1915–1916 for five months, and finally decided at the end of 1917 to come and settle in Calcutta and try to set up a practice. She took a small house in Elgin Road for a year, and was appointed doctor to the Diocesan College just opposite, but she was not happy in Calcutta. At the end of 1918 she applied for and obtained the post of Medical Officer at Jammu, Kashmir, for six months, and from there she went as a doctor to the Maharanis of Jind. But her health gave her ever-increasing trouble and she finally suspected that her digestive troubles were due to some sort of intestinal obstruction. She paid a short visit to Calcutta in 1919, but would not have herself examined or take any kind of treatment. On her return to Jind she was very poorly, and finally, after a very bad attack, was taken to a nursing home in Lahore in September 1920, where the doctor took a very grave view of her condition and wired the family in Calcutta to come at once. Milly prepared to start off at once with our cousin Satish Mookerjee but before they could start a telegram arrived on the 25th to say all was over. She was buried in the Lahore Cemetery.

Her character has already been well described by her lifelong friend Grace Alexander. In spite of her sharp tongue and critical attitude she was, at heart, the kindest and most charitable of women. She was a devout and enthusiastic Anglo Catholic and a regular Communicant, and took great pleasure in choral services with plenty of ritual. I too enjoyed such services and we went to as many as we could together, both at St. Michael's, Croydon, and afterwards at St. James, Calcutta. It is very sad to think that she never succeeded in her aim of setting up a practice of her own. Her life was much disturbed by her constant journeys between England and India as our father's companion, and in England later on, her nationality prevented her from entering into a partnership with other medical women, as they preferred to take English partners, and the same difficulty held as regards hospital appointments. In India, she was handicapped by her English upbringing and lack of familiarity with the vernacular of the places she was in, and also by her health. During the war, in 1915, and between her visits to India, she obtained the post of Home Surgeon in a Bristol Hospital for six months, and was very happy with that work. But it was only a temporary post, and she had to give it up.

Susie had many devoted friends besides Grace Alexander and always kept in touch with them. She and Miss Neligan were very fond of each other and she would visit Miss Neligan regularly till the latter died in 1913. Colonel Sinha and his family were close friends, and also Mr N.P. Gupta. Mary Jones was another friend, and Miss Bullock of Cambridge, and the Hoare family at Croydon. She took a real interest in all her nephews and nieces, and was very fond of them.

She left her money partly to be divided among her brothers and sisters, and partly to charities, one of which took the form of a scholarship for Indian women to take a teachers' training course in England, and this has been, and still is, a most successful enterprise.

3.5

Early School Days
P.M.'s Activities

Tara was a rather delicate child. She had whooping cough very badly at the age of two and this was followed by double pneumonia, and though she made a splendid recovery, she later used to get attacks of fever. Jai too caught everything that was going—chicken pox, whooping cough, etc., and used to get fits of asthma, so they did not go to school until Tara was eight and Jai 6½. Karun was a very healthy child, so when they first went to school he went also, though just five years old. They were sent to the Diocesan School, Calcutta, kept by the clever sisters, the sister in charge then being Sister Mary Victoria (now Miss Branson). She was a woman of outstanding personality and worked up the school from a small Mission School for Indian Christians to a big High School, to which non-Christian girls were eager to be admitted. She also opened a College Department (now closed) and had a large staff of English university women as lecturers as well as Indian graduates. When Tara first went to School in 1918, the staff included Ethel and Hilda Jackson, Maud Ebbutt and Miss Sanctuary, with all of whom we became very friendly. The kindergarten was in the charge of a Miss Daltry. Tara hated school at first, partly because she found lessons given in Bengali so difficult; all or most of the other children always spoke Bengali at home and had no difficulty in following. Jai and Karun enjoyed it because their cousins Dilip and Anil were also there. There is a story told of Tara refusing to go to school one day, and when forced to go, coming home on the back of the carriage! Somewhat exaggerated perhaps, but true in substance. However, she liked it better afterwards, and they all continued to attend school till we left Calcutta for good in 1920.

In the meantime the War went on and on, and seemed as if it would never end. Kalyan Mookerjee, who joined up in 1914 as a Captain in the Indian Medical Service, was sent to Mesopotamia, taken prisoner at the fall of Kut-el-Amara, and died of typhus in a Turkish prison. This was a most terrible blow to his poor wife Bibha (a niece of the Maharani of Cooch Behar), more especially as her only child had died of dysentery not long before. Other friends had joined up and been killed. Nearly all the young men who had been my contemporaries at Cambridge, even the most revolutionary and 'Fabian'[71] of them, had joined up at once and very few seemed to come back. Amongst these were Bill Hubbock, Mr Keeling, and Rupert Brooke, the poet. Kew, who had won a scholarship from Bilton Grange to Rugby, and an open scholarship from Rugby to New College, Oxford, joined the Royal Flying Corps as it was then called and was sent to India, to Rissalpur. He spent a few days in Calcutta to his mother's extreme pleasure, for she said she had never in her wildest dreams imagined him coming back to Calcutta as an Air Force Officer! Laddie Roy, the second son of our friend Mr P.L. Roy, also joined the R.F.C. and did brilliantly but was killed. He got the D.F.C. posthumously. Peter Sen's son Mickey was another Airman. When the Indian Air Force was formed in 1933, with three Bengalis among the first nine officers (Sircar, Subrata Mookerjee, and Karun Majumdar), it was interesting to find that the earliest Indian officers during the War had also been Bengalis.

The story of India's participation in the War has been told too often to need repetition here, and the doings of the Bengali Infantry Regiment and the Labour Corps (led by Father Douglass) are well known.[72] In 1914 some keen spirits including P.M., Omi Chaudhuri, and H.M. Bose, with the help of Colonel Pugh, who founded the Bengali Light Horse, and worked very hard indeed to make this a satisfactory and well-trained unit. They went into Camp in 1918, and were secretly somewhat disappointed when the Armistice was declared before they had a chance of showing the mettle of their pastures. P.M. had been a keen volunteer in the Warwickshire Regiment when he was at college in Birmingham. Later on, in 1924, on the strength if this experience and the Bengal Light Horse training, he joined the Army in India Reserve of

Officers (A.I.R.O.) as Lieutenant and obtained his promotion to Captain in 1932 before he had to retire (owing to the age limit) in 1934.

We were at Simultala in the Autumn of 1918 when the Armistice was declared, and liked the place so much that we bought some land there, intending to build a house; and our cook, Harvey Singh, who had been with us since our marriage, also bought a plot of land there! Simultala is near Gidhaur, and P.M. enjoyed being in that neighborhood and went over one day to see the Maharaja, who helped us in acquiring the land.

On our return to Calcutta at the end of November 1918, we all went down with influenza which was then raging in epidemic form all over the world, and was called 'War Fever'. We were all five ill at the same time, but P.M.'s attack was the worst, as his head was affected. Our doctor then was a relative, Dr Amiya Madhub Mallik, whose daughter married P.M.'s nephew Pinu. Though a fully trained allopathic doctor and a gold medallist, he had taken to homeopathy and made us all temporary converts. P.M. was kept in bed for some time as one of his heart-sounds was wrong. He bore this patiently for some time, and then one day sent me out for a drive and surreptitiously went and played Polo and came back to bed, and that evening the doctor found his 'heart sound' miraculously improved! But he had to be very careful for some time.

3.6

Goodbye to Calcutta
1919–20

We had for a long time been wanting to buy a house in Darjeeling, to solve the problem of where to go every pujah holiday, and in 1919 we heard of the land called 'Point Clear' quite by chance, through Mr Sailen Banerjee. This land belonged to his father Mr Mahendra Banerji, Government Pleader, Darjeeling. There had been a house there, but it had fallen down in the 1897 earthquake and the land had been condemned, but Mr Banerji assured us that it was really perfectly safe and was now passed as fit for building purposes. About the same time we were lucky in getting a good offer for 1 Elysium Row, and had already built houses at 7 Bright Street and Burdwan Road, Alipore. We had to leave 1 Elysium Row in April 1919, so decided to go to Darjeeling and see about Mr Banerji's land. We took 'Kilfane Lodge' for a year, and stayed there from April to the end of June, and again for September and October and part of November. We inspected the land and found it an ideal site, and had it tested and approved by various engineers and other authorities, and finally bought in the autumn of 1919. The building was begun at once by the 'General Engineering Company', Darjeeling—two brothers H.S. Roy and B.B. Roy. P.M. drew up the plans himself, having had a good deal of experience after designing two houses in Calcutta. We went down to Calcutta in November, and came up again in April 1920 and stayed at 'Ahentully II' to be near the new house. P.M. was not able to be there the whole time, but came up for a few days every now and then, and Mrs Mason stayed with me. 'Point Clear' was more or less completed in August 1920, and we moved in on the 29 August, knowing that the house would never really be finished to our liking unless we were actually living there. That same year the Chaudhuris bought 'The Wigwam' to live in, and the two adjoining houses, 'Dant Koti' and 'Ida Villa', for letting purposes. The Bonnerjees also came up that summer to stay at Mrs R.N. Roy's house 'Roseville,' so there was a gathering of the clans. Tara and Jai and Karun began going to the Maharani School for some hours every day. This school was founded by Mrs B.B. Sarkar with the help of the Maharanis of Burdwan, Cooch Behar, and Mourbhurg. Mrs Sarkar, daughter of the famous Pandit Siva Nath Sastri, who was one of the very earliest Brahmos, is a pioneer of Bengali women's education, being herself a highly educated and cultured woman. She married Dr B.B. Sarkar who settled in Darjeeling for his health and established a practice here. There was at that time no school here for Indian girls, and they were taken, more or less on sufferance, as day girls only at the Loreto Convent. Having three daughters of her own to be educated, and wanting them to have an education on Indian lines, Mrs Sarkar decided to open a small school for Indian girls, and as has been said, the three Maharanis offered their help. The School began in a very small way in 1908 in one room on Mackenzie Road with half-a-dozen children and four or five teachers. But it grew so rapidly that very soon a house was taken for it and an appeal made for a Government Grant which was given at once. This house, 'Oak Lodge', belonged to the Cooch Behar State and was never very convenient for the ever-increasing numbers of day girls and small boys and boarders. The standard of the School was so high, and the examination results so uniformly successful—the percentage of passes in the Calcutta matric being usually cent per cent, and every year one or more Government Scholarships being obtained by the girls—that the Government promised a large grant of Rs 50,000 towards the purchase of suitable premises, if the School Committee could raise a like amount. The School Committee had done its part, and a suitable plot of land had been purchased at 'Orchid Lee' below the railway station. But the Government has so far only been able to subscribe Rs 10,000 out of the promised amount owing to the slump and consequent retrenchment of education grants, so the building cannot be begun, and the School, which now has over 200 scholars and a waiting list, has to be carried on in a most inconvenient way in a small dwelling house and a number of sheds. The examination results, however, are just as good as before despite these drawbacks, and for two years running—1934 and 1935—the School has sent up the girl who won the Keshub Sen Gold Medal for coming first in the whole Province.

Editor's Note

The following lines appear almost as some last-minute thoughts at the end of Janaki Majumdar's Family History. *Unfortunately, the page from the diary—which might have conveyed the belated character of their appearance—was too light to be scanned. I have nonetheless decided to include these apparent after-thoughts at the end of this volume in order to remain faithful to the diary in its original form.*

A chapter on the Bonnerjee and Chaudhuri children, etc.
Kali's marriage and child. Rangoon.
Majumdar relations.
Books read and enjoyed.
Parties adult and children.

W.C. Bonnerjee—Some Recollections of a Daughter
My father was born in 1844 and was in his middle forties when I was born, so my first recollections of him are as a tall awe-inspiring figure with a long beard already going grey. His children were brought up in England and all we saw of him was in the long vacation when he used to come to England and take all his large family for wonderful holidays. He used to love telling us stories of his early life, that he was a lazy pleasure-loving boy and how deplorably he wasted his time at school though he had a flair for passing examinations.

Notes

[1] John Henry Tull Walsh, *A History of Murshidabad District, Bengal. With Biographies of Some of its Noted Families* (London: Jarrold & Sons, 1902).

[2] Not macadamized, i.e., untarred.

[3] Hired carriage.

[4] Originally a Moghul term, 'Bahadur' was the official title of members of the second class of the Order of the British Empire in India; 'Rai Bahadur' was also conferred upon Hindu civil officers. See Henry Yule and A.C. Burnell (eds), *Hobson-Jobson: A Glossary of Colloquial Anglo-Indian Words and Phrases ...* [1886] (New Delhi: Rupa and Co., 1994), p. 48.

[5] Though his initials were technically 'P.K.' (for Prio Krishnar), Janaki refers to him as 'P.M.' throughout the manuscript.

[6] Grooms.

[7] Mail (in this case, probably delivery or pick-up).

[8] This is an abbreviation for 'tattoo', a native-bred pony; see Yule and Burnell, *Hobson-Jobson*, p. 902.

[9] A boy employed by a household (or a regiment).

[10] Present or gift, made by an inferior to a superior, usually in anticipation of largesse.

[11] The most decorated part (the end) of the sari, which a woman would use to cover her head with if she wanted to be modest.

[12] This is blank in the original manuscript.

[13] Chokidar; watchman.

[14] Outhouse of an élite home; the boundary beyond which outsiders are not allowed; the border between 'home' and 'world', in the Tagorean sense.

[15] A milk sweet.

[16] Subodh was also a financial backer of the newspaper *Bande Mataram* and a friend of Aurobindo Ghose. See Leonard Gordon, *Bengal: The Nationalist Movement 1876–1940* (New Delhi: Manohar, 1979), p. 116.

[17] Sen (1838–1884) was a prominent Brahmo Samajist; see Meredith Borthwick, *Keshub Chunder Sen: A Search for Cultural Synthesis* (Calcutta: Minerva Associates, 1977).

[18] Pulmonary tuberculosis.

[19] Sunity Devi (1864–1932). See Biswanath Das (ed.), *Autobiography of an Indian Princess: Memoirs of Maharani Sunity Devi of Cooch Behar* (New Delhi: Vikas, 1995).

[20] Satyendra Prasanna Sinha (1864–1928); barrister; Congress President (1915); later Undersecretary of State for India; see Gordon, *Bengal*, p. 21.

[21] For accounts of Indian student-life in Victorian Britain see Rozina Visram, *Ayahs, Lascars and Princes: The Story of Indians in Britain, 1700–1947* (London: Pluto, 1986); Antoinette Burton, *At the Heart of the Empire: Indians and the Colonial Encounter in Late-Victorian Britain* (Berkeley: University of California Press, 1998); Shompa Lahiri, *Indians in Britain: Anglo-Indian Encounters, Race and Identity, 1880–1930* (London: Frank Cass, 2000); and Rozina Visram, *Asians in Britain: 400 Years of History* (London: Pluto, 2002).

[22] I.A. is 'Intermediate Arts'—the first examination conducted by the universities following two years of education after 10th standard. Then students were admitted to a two-year (pass course) or three-year (Honours course) B.A. 'Matric' is the exam given at the end of 10 years' schooling.

[23] Lower level judgeship; at the bottom of the judicial hierarchy; overseeing civil matters, usually at the district level.

[24] See also Sadhona Bonnerjee, *Life of W.C. Bonnerjee, First President of the Indian National Congress* (Calcutta, n.d. [*c*. 1944]).

[25] From the Persian, meaning scribe; lawyer, advocate.

[26] Typically, *mukhteer*: a pleader who did not have a law degree but only a license to plead in court.

[27] A traditional Hindu village school. For a historical account of pathsalas which draws on autobiographical accounts see Gautam Chando Roy, 'The Pathsala and the School: Experiences of Growing up in Nineteenth and Twentieth Century Bengal', in Rajat Kanta Ray (ed.), *Mind, Body and Society: Life and Mentality in Colonial Bengal* (Calcutta: Oxford University Press, 1995), pp. 195–231.

[28] Doorkeeper.

[29] One sixteenth of a rupee.

[30] Light meals; snacks.

[31] From the Sanskrit, idol or deity; term of respect (also a Kshatriya caste).

[32] For a discussion of the value attached to female beauty among Bengali bhadralok see Dipesh Chakrabarty, *Provincializing Europe: Postcolonial Thought and Historical Difference* (New Jersey: Princeton University Press, 2000), chapter 8.

[33] See Lahiri, *Indians in Britain*, p. 66.

[34] Black waters.

[35] For a more detailed account of this story see Manickal Mukherjee, *W.C. Bonnerjee: Snapshots from his Life and Letters* (Calcutta: Deshbandu Book Depot, 1949).

[36] This sentence is crossed out in the original.

[37] 1848–1925; Congress President 1895, 1902; see his memoir, *A Nation in Making: Being the Reminiscences of Persons, Things, English and India...* [1925] (Calcutta: Oxford University Press, 1963).

[38] Roger Manvell, *The Trial of Annie Besant and Charles Bradlaugh* (New York: Horizon Press, 1976).

[39] Society for the Promotion of Christian Knowledge.

[40] 1844–1896; barrister of Calcutta High Court; see S.R. Mehrotra, *The Emergence of the Indian National Congress* (Delhi: Vikas, 1971), p. 165.

[41] This is the same group to which Edmond Gosse and his family belonged. In fact, Gosse records meeting an 'Asiatic' lady at one of the meetings (she was married to an Irishman so it was not likely to have been Hemangini). See his *Father and Son* (New York: W.W. Norton, 1963), pp. 11 and 44.

[42] For an account of the challenges of raising boys in "new" nationalist households see Pradip Kumar Bose, 'Sons of the Nation: Child Rearing in the New Family', in Partha Chatterjee (ed.), *Texts of Power: Emerging Disciplines in Bengal* (Minneapolis: University of Minnesota Press, 1995), pp. 118–44.

[43] For an account of some of his early cases see Bonnerjee, *Life of W.C. Bonnerjee*, pp. 22–5.

[44] *Ibid.*, p. 104.

[45] The final rites for Brahmins, Baidyas, Kayasthas and other 'higher caste people', performed on the eleventh day after a natural (versus untimely) death; often done yearly on the anniversary of the person's death.

[46] For accounts of the founding years of the Indian National Congres see Martin Briton, *New India: 1885* (Berkeley: University of California Press, 1969); Mehrotra, *Emergence of the Indian National Congress*; Sumit Sarkar, *Modern*

India: 1885–1947 (Madras: Macmillan, 1983), especially chapters 2 and 3; Iqbal Singh, *Indian National Congress: A Reconstruction, 1885–1918*, vol. 1(New Delhi: Nehru Memorial Museum and Library, 1988); and John R. McLane, 'The Early Congress, Hindu Populism, and the Wider Society', in Richard Sisson and Stanley Wolpert (eds), *Congress and Indian Nationalism: The Pre-Independence Phase* (Berkeley: University of California Press, 1988), pp. 47–61. For the history of the INC in Britain see Margot D., Morrow, 'The Origins and Early Years of the British Committee of the Indian National Congress, 1885–1907' (Ph.D. dissertation, University of London, 1977).

[47] See Edwin Hirschmann, *'White Mutiny': The Ilbert Bill Crisis in India and the Genesis of the Indian National Congress* (Columbia, Missouri: South Asia Books, 1980); Mrinalini Sinha, ' 'Chathams, Pitts and Gladstones in Petticoats': The Politics of Gender and Race in the Ilbert Bill Controversy, 1883–1884', in Nupur Chaudhuri and Margaret Strobel (eds), *Western Women and Imperialism: Complicity and Resistance* (Bloomington and Indianapolis: Indiana University Press, 1992), pp. 98–118; and Chandrika Kaul, 'England and India: the Ilbert Bill, 1883: A Case Study of the Metropolitan Press', in *Indian Economic and Social History Review* 30 (1993): 412–36.

[48] For a reprint of the official 1885 INC Resolutions see W.C. Bonnerjee (ed.), *Indian Politics* (Madras: G.A. Natesan, 1898).

[49] For details see Bonnerjee, *The Life of W.C. Bonnerjee*.

[50] This reads like a *Who's Who* of this first generation of Indian nationalists; see Gordon, *Bengal*; Mehrotra, *Emergence*; and Visram, *Asians in Britain*.

[51] For a detailed account of Indians at Oxbridge see Paul Deslandes, 'The Foreign Element: Newcomers and the Rhetoric of Race, Nation, and Empire in "Oxbridge" Undergraduate Culture, 1850–1920', in *Journal of British Studies* 37, 1(1998).

[52] For an account of Victorian indoor plumbing see Sally Mitchell, *Daily Life in Victorian England* (Connecticut: Greenwood Press, 1996); for an overview of Victorian domestic architecture, more generally, see Lynne Walker, 'Home Making: An Architectural Perspective', in *Signs* 27, 3 (Connecticut, 2002); 823–846.

[53] For some historical accounts of the shifting contexts of hearth and home in India see Sambuddha Chakrabarty, 'Changing Notions of Conjugal Relations in Nineteenth Century Bengal' and Judith Walsh, 'The Virtuous Wife and the Well-ordered Home: The Reconceptualization of Bengali Women and their Worlds', both in Ray (ed.), *Mind, Body and Society*, pp. 297–330 and 331–63, respectively. See also Judith Walsh, 'What Women Learned When Men Gave

them Advice: Re-Writing Patrirachy in Late-Ninteenth Century Bengal', *Journal of Asian Studies* 56, 3 (1997): 641–77.

⁵⁴John Coffey, 'Democracy and Popular Religion: Moody and Sankey's Mission to Britain, 1873–75', in Eugenio F. Biagini (ed.), *Citizenship and Community: Liberals, Radicals and Collective Identities in the British Isles, 1865–1931* (Cambridge: Cambridge University Press, 1996).

⁵⁵1848–1909; Congress President, 1898; for a recent evaluation of his nationalist activities see Henry Schwarz, *Writing Cultural History in Colonial and Postcolonial India* (Philadelphia : University of Pennsylvania Press, 1997).

⁵⁶Footnote by Janaki Agnes Penelope Majumdar: 'Miss Grace Harling, as she then was, was a very beautiful girl with lovely dark hair and eyes, a beautiful complexion and a very sweet expression. She was so lovely that ...' [text trails off].

⁵⁷For two accounts of English women's medical work in India see Margaret Balfour and Ruth Young, *The Medical Work of Women in India* (London: Oxford University Press, 1929); Geraldine Forbes, 'Medical Careers and Health Care for Indian Women', in *Women's History Review* 3, 4 (1994): 515–30.

⁵⁸See Visram, *Asians in Britain*, p. 163.

⁵⁹For a detailed analysis of servant life in Calcutta in this period see Swapna Mitra Bannerjee, *Middle Class Women and Domestics in Colonial Calcutta, 1900–1947* (Ph.D. dissertation, Temple University, 1998).

⁶⁰See Felicity Hunt. (ed.), *Lessons for Life: The Schooling of Girls and Women, 1850–1950* (Oxford: Basil Blackwell, 1987).

⁶¹See S.B. Cook, *Imperial Affinities: Nineteenth Century Analogies and Exchanges between India and Ireland* (New Delhi: Sage, 1993).

⁶²These were two pioneers of women in medicine and women's suffrage, respectively; see Philippa Levine, *Victorian Feminism 1850–1900* (Tallahassee: Florida State University Press, 1987).

⁶³See Edith Moberly Bell, *Storming the Citadel: The Rise of the Woman Doctor* (London: Constable, 1953); Catriona Blake, *The Charge of the Parasols: Women's Entry into the Medical Profession* (London: Women's Press, 1990); Antoinette Burton, 'Contesting the Zenana: The Mission to Make "Lady Doctors for India", 1874–1885', *Journal of British Studies* 35 (1996): 368–97.

⁶⁴One of the founders of the Congress Political Agency in Britain; see Visram, *Asians in Britain*, p. 125.

⁶⁵For an account of other Indian parliamentarians, would-be and successful, see Visram, *Ayahs*; Visram, *Asians in Britain*; and Antoinette Burton, 'Tongues

Untied: Lord Salisbury's "Black Man" and the Boundaries of Imperial Democracy', in *Comparative Studies in Society and History* (2000) 43, 2: 632–59.

⁶⁶Gopal Krishna Gokhale (1866–1915); advocate of moderate political action; secretary of the Poona Sarvajanik Sabha.

⁶⁷This is crossed out in the original.

⁶⁸The NIA dated from the Victorian era; see Burton, *At the Heart of the Empire*, chapter 1.

⁶⁹See Susan Leonardi, *Dangerous by Degrees: Women at Oxford and the Somerville College Novelists* (New Brunswick: Rutgers University Press, 1989).

⁷⁰For Fawcett, a suffragist, see David Rubinstein, *A Different World for Women: The Life of Millicent Garrett* (Columbus: Ohio State University Press, 1991).

⁷¹That is, of the Fabian Society, a socialist group in Britain which included Sydney and Beatrice Webb.

⁷²See Visram, *Asians in Britain*, pp. 169–95 and David Ormissi (ed.), *Indian Voices of the Great War* (London: Macmillan, 1999).

Select Bibliography

Amin, Sonia. 'Childhood and Role Models in the Andar Mahal: Muslim Women in the Private Sphere in Colonial Bengal', in Kumari Jayawardena and Malathi de Alwis (eds), *Embodied Violence: Communalising Women's Sexuality in South Asia*, London: Zed Books, 1996, pp. 71–8.

Bannerjee, Himani. 'Fashioning a Self: Gender, Class and Moral Education for and by Women in Colonial Bengal', in Kate Rousmanière et al. (eds), *Discipline, Moral Regulation and Schooling: A Social History*, New York: Garland, 1997, pp. 183–218.

―――― . Shahrzad Mojab and Judith Whitehead (eds), *Of Property and Propriety: The Role of Gender and Class in Imperialism and Nationalism*, University of Toronto Press, 2001.

Bonnerjee, Sadhona. *Life of W.C. Bonnerjee, First President of the Indian National Congress*, [c. 1944], Calcutta, n.d.

Bonnerjee, W.C. (ed.), *Indian Politics*, Madras: G.A. Natesan, 1898.

Borthwick, Meredith. *Keshub Chunder Sen: A Search for Cultural Synthesis*, Calcutta: Minerva Associates, 1977.

Bose, Pradip Kumar. 'Sons of the Nation: Child Rearing in the New Family', in Partha Chatterjee (ed.), *Texts of Power: Emerging Disciplines in Colonial Bengal*, University of Minnesota Press, 1995, pp. 118–44.

Burton, Antoinette. *At the Heart of the Empire: Indians and the Colonial Encounter in Late-Victorian Britain*, Berkeley: University of California Press, 1998.

―――― . *Burdens of History: British Feminists, Indian Women and Imperial Culture, 1865–1915*, University of North Carolina Press, 1994.

―――― . *Dwelling in the Archive: Women Writing House, Home and History in Late-Colonial India*, New York: Oxford University Press, 2003.

―――― . 'From Child Bride to "Hindoo Lady": Rukhmabai and the Debate on Sexual Respectability in Imperial Britain', in *American Historical Review* 103, 4 (1998): 1119–46.

———. 'Tongues Untied: Lord Salisbury's "Black Man" and the Boundaries of Imperial Democracy', in *Comparative Studies in Society and History* 43, 2 (2000): 632–59.

Chakrabarty, Dipesh. 'The Difference-Deferral of (A) Colonial Modernity: Public Debates on Domesticity in British Bengal', in *History Workshop Journal* 36 (1993): 1–33.

———. *Provincializing Europe: Postcolonial Thought and Historical Difference*, Princeton University Press, 2000.

Chakravarti, Uma. *Rewriting History: The Life and Times of Pandita Ramabai*, New Delhi: Kali for Women, 1998.

Chandra, Sudhir. *Enslaved Daughters: Colonialism, Law and Women's Rights*, Delhi: Oxford University Press, 1998.

Chatterjee, Partha. 'The Nationalist Resolution of the Woman Question', in Kumkum Sangari and Sudesh Vaid (eds), *Recasting Women: Essays in Colonial History*, Delhi: Kali for Women, 1989, pp. 233–53.

Cook, S.B. *Imperial Affinities: Nineteenth Century Analogies and Exchanges between India and Ireland*, New Delhi: Sage, 1993.

Davidoff, Leonore and Catherine Hall, *Family Fortunes*, University of Chicago Press, 1987.

Das, Biswanath (ed.), *Autobiography of an Indian Princess: Memoirs of Maharani Sunity Devi of Cooch Behar*, New Delhi: Vikas, 1995.

Deslandes, Paul. '"The Foreign Element": Newcomers and the Rhetoric of Race, Nation, and Empire in "Oxbridge" Undergraduate Culture, 1850–1920', in *Journal of British Studies* 37, 1(1998).

Forbes, Geraldine. 'Goddesses or Rebels? The Women Revolutionaries of Bengal', *The Oracle* 11, 2 (April 1980): 1–15.

———. *The New Cambridge History of India: Women in Modern India*, Cambridge University Press, 1996.

——— (ed.), *An Indian Freedom Fighter Recalls Her Life* by Manmohini Zutshi Saghal, New York: M.E. Sharpe, 1994.

——— (ed.), *Memoirs of an Indian Woman* by Shudha Mazumdar, New York: M.E. Sharpe, 1989.

——— and Tapan Raychaudhuri (eds), *From Child Widow to Lady Doctor: The Memoirs of Dr. Haimabati Sen*, New Delhi: Roli Books, 2000.

Gandhi, Mohandas K. *An Autobiography; or the Story of My Experiments with Truth* [1927], Ahmedabad: Navijivan Publishing House, 1990 rpt.

Gordon, Leonard. *Bengal: The Nationalist Movement 1876–1940*, New Delhi: Manohar, 1979.

Grewal, Inderpal. *Home and Harem: Nation, Gender, Empire and the Cultures of Travel*, Durham: Duke University Press, 1996.

Kosambi, Meera. 'The Meeting of the Twain: The Cultural Confrontation of Three Women in Nineteenth Century Maharashtra', in *Indian Journal of Gender Studies* 1, 1 (1994): 1–22.

———— (ed.), *Pandita Ramabai Through Her Own Words—Selected Works*, Delhi: Oxford University Press, 2000.

Kumar, Radha. *The History of Doing*, London: Verso, 1994.

Lahiri, Shompa. *Indians in Britain: Anglo-Indian Encounters, Race and Identity, 1880–1930*, London: Frank Cass, 2000.

Lokugé, Chandani (ed.), *India Calling: The Memories of Cornelia Sorabji, India's First Woman Barrister*, Delhi: Oxford University Press, 2001.

Mani, Lata. *Contentious Traditions: The Debate on Sati in Colonial India*, Berkeley: University of California, 1998.

Masselos, Jim. *Towards Nationalism: Group Affiliations and the Politics of Public Associations in Nineteenth Century Western India*, Bombay: Popular Prakashan, 1974.

Mehrotra, S.R. *The Emergence of the Indian National Congress*, Delhi: Vikas, 1971.

Mukherjee, Manickal. *W.C. Bonnerjee: Snapshots from his Life and Letters*, Calcutta: Deshbandu Book Depot, 1949.

Mukherjee, Nilmani (ed.), *A Bengal Zamindar: Jaykrishna Mukherjee of Uttarpara and His Times, 1808–1888*, Calcutta: Firma K.L. Mukhopadhyay, 1975.

Ormissi, David (ed.), *Indian Voices of the Great War*, London: Macmillan, 1999.

Rao, Anu (ed.), *Caste, Gender and Indian Feminism*, Delhi: Kali for Women, forthcoming.

Rao, Uma. 'Women in the Frontline: The Case of U.P.', in Leela Kasturi and Vina Mazumdar (eds), *Women and Indian Nationalism*, New Delhi: Vikas, 1994, pp. 28–52.

Ray, Bharati. 'Calcutta Women in the Swadeshi Movement (1903–1910): The Nature and Implications of Participation', in Pradip Sinha (ed.), *The Urban Experience: Calcutta*, Calcutta: Riddhi, 1987, pp. 168–81.

Roy, Gautam Chando. 'The Pathsala and the School: Experiences of Growing up in Nineteenth and Twentieth Century Bengal', in Rajat Kanta Ray (ed.), *Mind, Body and Society: Life and Mentality in Colonial Bengal*, Calcutta: Oxford University Press, 1995, pp. 195–231.

Sarkar, Sumit. *Modern India, 1885–1947*, New Delhi: Macmillan, 1983.

Sarkar, Tanika. *Hindu Wife, Hindu Nation: Community, Religion and Cultural Nationalism*, Delhi: Permanent Black, 2001.

———. *Words to Win: The Making of Amar Jiban: A Modern Autobiography*, New Delhi: Kali for Women, 1999.

Schwarz, Henry. *Writing Cultural History in Colonial and Postcolonial India*, Philadelphia: University of Pennsylvania Press, 1997.

Seal, Anil. *The Emergence of Indian Nationalism: Competition and Collaboration in the Later Nineteenth Century*, Cambridge University Press, 1968.

Seth, Sanjay. 'Rewriting Histories of Nationalism: The Politics of "Moderate Nationalism" in India, 1870–1905', in *American Historical Review* 104, 1 (February 1999): 95–116.

Singh, Hari Lal. *Problems and Policies of the British in India, 1885–1898*, New York: Asia Publishing House, 1963.

Singh, Iqbal. *Indian National Congress: A Reconstruction, 1885–1918*, vol. 1, New Delhi: Nehru Memorial Museum and Library, 1988.

Sinha, Mrinalini. '"Chathams, Pitts and Gladstones in Petticoats": The Politics of Gender and Race in the Ilbert Bill Controversy, 1883–1884', in Nupur Chaudhuri and Margaret Strobel (eds), *Western Women and Imperialism: Complicity and Resistance*, Bloomington and Indianapolis: Indiana University Press, 1992, pp. 98–118.

———. 'The Lineage of the "Indian" Modern: Rhetoric, Agency, and the Sarda Act in Late Colonial India', in Antoinette Burton (ed.), *Gender, Sexuality and Colonial Modernities*, London: Routledge, 1999, pp. 207–21.

———. 'Refashioning Mother India: Feminism and Nationalism in Late-Colonial India', *Feminist Studies* 28, 3 (Fall 2000): 623–44.

———. (ed.), *Mother India*, Delhi: Kali for Women, 1998, Ann Arbor: University of Michigan Press, 2000.

Sisson, Richard and Stanley Wolpert (eds), *Congress and Indian Nationalism: The Pre-Independence Phase*, Berkeley: University of California Press, 1988.

Sunder Rajan, Rajeswari (ed.), *Signposts: Gender Issues in Post-Independence India*, New Delhi: Kali for Women, 1999.

Tharu, Susie and K Lalita (eds), *Women Writing in India: 600 BC to the Present*, vols 1 and 2, New York: The Feminist Press, 1991.

Visweswaran, Kamala. 'Small Speeches, Subaltern Gender: Nationalist Ideology and its Historiography', in Shahid Amin and Dipesh Chakrabarty (eds), *Subaltern Studies IX*, Delhi: Oxford University Press, 1996, pp. 83–125.

Walsh, Judith. 'The Virtuous Wife and the Well-Ordered Home: The Reconceptuialization of Bengali Women and their Worlds', in Rajat Kanta Ray (ed.), *Mind, Body and Society: Life and Mentality in Colonial Bengal*, Calcutta: Oxford University Press, 1995, pp. 331–63.

———. 'What Women Learned When Men Gave Them Advice: Re-writing Patriarchy in Late-Nineteenth Century Bengal', in *Journal of Asian Studies* 56, 3 (1997): 641–77.

Wolpert, Stanley. *Tilak and Gokhale: Revolution and Reform in the Making of Modern India*, Berkeley: University of California Press, 1962.